Making Your Heart's Truth into Literature

The Passionate, Accurate Story

Also by Carol Bly:

The Tomcat's Wife and Other Stories

Soil and Survival:
Land Stewardship and the Future of American Agriculture
(with Joe Paddock and Nancy Paddock)

Bad Government and Silly Literature

Backbone

Letters from the Country

Making Your Heart's Truth into Literature

The Passionate, Accurate Story

CAROL BLY

M I L K W E E D   E D I T I O N S

Published 1998 by Milkweed Editions
Printed in the United States of America
Cover design by Sally Wagner
Cover photo by PhotoDisc, Inc.
Interior design by Randy Scholes
The text of this book is set in ITC Garamond
98 99 00 01 02   5 4 3 2 1
First Edition

Milkweed Editions is a not-for-profit publisher. Original publication of this book was funded by contributions from the I. A. O'Shaughnessy Foundation, and with support from the Literature Program of the National Endowment for the Arts; Arts Development Fund of United Arts; Dayton Hudson Foundation for Dayton's and Target Stores; First Bank System Foundation; General Mills Foundation; Jerome Foundation; Minnesota State Arts Board through an appropriation by the Minnesota State Legislature; Northwest Area Foundation; and by the support of generous individuals. This edition of the book was made possible in part by additional funds from the Elmer L. and Eleanor J. Andersen Foundation; James Ford Bell Foundation; Bush Foundation; Cray Research, a Silicon Graphics Company; Dayton's, Mervyn's, and Target Stores by the Dayton Hudson Foundation; Doherty, Rumble and Butler Foundation; Honeywell Foundation; The McKnight Foundation; Andrew W. Mellon Foundation; Challenge and Creation and Presentation Programs of the National Endowment for the Arts; Norwest Foundation on behalf of Norwest Bank Minnesota, Norwest Investment Management & Trust, Lowry Hill, Norwest Investment Services, Inc.; Lawrence and Elizabeth Ann O'Shaughnessy Charitable Income Trust in honor of Lawrence M. O'Shaughnessy; Piper Jaffray Companies, Inc.; Ritz Foundation; John and Beverly Rollwagen Fund of the Minneapolis Foundation; The St. Paul Companies, Inc.; James R. Thorpe Foundation; and by the support of generous individuals.

Library of Congress Cataloging-in-Publication Data
Bly, Carol
    The passionate, accurate story / by Carol Bly.
        p.   cm.
    ISBN 1-57131-219-6
    I. English language—Rhetoric—Study and teaching. 2. Creative writing—Study and teaching. I. Title.
    PE1404.B59   1990
    808.3—dc20   90-4119
                                                                                    CIP

This book is printed on acid-free paper.

for Donald Hall

ACKNOWLEDGEMENTS

I am indebted to these people for helping me develop my materials: Patricia Hampl, Phebe Hanson, and Sonia Matison. I am grateful to Bob Perlongo of *Triquarterly* magazine for permission to use a passage from *Triquarterly 75: Writing and Well-being*, "Writing from the Darkness" by Bell Hooks.

Contents

INTRODUCTION *Writing Whole Literature / 1*

Jill's Wrath: How We Treat Young Writers / 1

Ugly Facts of Our Time and Our Sense of the
Public Concern / 9

CHAPTER ONE *First Draft Work Is Like No Other Work
in the Story / 18*

The Approach of Critics Is Not the Approach of
Writers / 18

The First Draft / 20

Leaving the *Donnée*: Inviting the
Unconscious / 22

Leaving the *Donnée* as a Form of Love of
the Universe / 30

CHAPTER TWO *How to Generate Not Words but
Emotional Content / 35*

Values Listing: Why Write One? / 38

Values Listing: Examples / 39

Writing a 3,000-to-10,000-Word
Autobiography / 41

The First Draft As Generation / 49

First Draft: Practicing Containment / 51

CHAPTER THREE   *Plot and Subplot / 54*

    Getting to Plot / 54

    Five Uses of Subplot / 61

CHAPTER FOUR   *The People / 69*

    Characters Made in the Usual Way / 69

    Characters Made out of Our Various Selves / 74

    Questions to Ask of the Characters / 82

    Management of Characters / 83

    Three Appearances of Each Character
    by Mention at Least / 90

    Point of View / 93

CHAPTER FIVE   *Chronology in the Short Story / 95*

    Leaving the First Draft: Working for Theater
    and Moral Intensity / 95

    The Strengths of Chronological Order
    in Stories / 103

    Introducing People Before Weather
    and Props / 105

    A Listing Format / 109

    "That Is the *First* Thing I Thought of: What Is
    the *Second?*" / 110

CHAPTER SIX   *Dialogue / 113*

    Keeping Good Tone Despite the Dialogue / 113

    Realism: Inner Versus Other / 115

    Dialogue As Exposition / 120

    Dialogue Has Its Own Devices / 123

    The Physical Building of Dialogue / 127

    An Argument Against Starting Stories
    with Dialogue / 131

CHAPTER SEVEN *How Stories Take Place in a Place / 133*

The Attractions of Having
No Physical Setting / 133

The Psychological Uses of Utopian Writing / 135

Physical Setting for Contrast / 138

Making Your Own Fresh Assessment of Places:
Eschewing Collective Opinion / 139

Periphery of Place: We May Be Neglecting It
in Order to Avoid Pain / 141

The Sense of History and of Future
in a Place / 145

CHAPTER EIGHT *Props Large and Small / 154*

Props and Tone / 154

Props and Clichés / 157

Small Props / 159

Props as the Fascinating Gear
of Others / 162

CHAPTER NINE *Small Cures / 170*

Surprise / 171

Plurals and Generics / 172

Anglo-Saxon and Latinate Words / 175

Soft or Stale Words / 180

Long and Short Sounds / 182

CHAPTER TEN *Our Tottering Plot / 184*

Solving for Plot Among Our Mixed Bag
of Characters / 184

Mapping / 186

Planning the Eventual Death of Each Character
for Plot Use and for Our Own Psychological
Clarity / 193

Saving What Doesn't Fit / 196

Writing Whole Literature: Writing the Good News As Well As the Psychological Dismay

Jill's Wrath: How We Treat Young Writers

The greatest beauty in a short story mainly floats towards us from its plot. That is not a fashionable idea just at the moment, but it is true. In Charles Baxter's "Scheherazade," an old woman is healing her husband. He is in the hospital, after a stroke.[1] She tells him tall stories which he experiences as empowering. We see what he needs: he needs to see himself as the ever-seductive male patrolling the range of does and mares, cutting his swath, a man with no consideration of any human being other than himself. His wife's stories are designed to reassure him that all that starry selfishness is intact. There is beauty in the language and structure, because Baxter is one of the most passionate and most subtle short-story writers of our time—but what makes me say, "What a beautiful story!" is Baxter's plot. This wife is not under threat of being killed if she can't amuse her husband, yet she is an echo of the original Scheherazade because she sacrifices her own psychological health—the sense of what is *fair and decent*—in order to return her husband to his health. The story has beauty of plot.

All beauty isn't in plot. There are two psychological disciplines authors exercise which make stories beautiful in tone and language: The first is the determination not to be embittered—at the same time as one avoids denial of the evil that people do. That is very difficult. It is hard to describe

1

wretched behavior in even the tiniest corner of life without cynicism, perhaps because people will likely continue to behave in the bad ways. The second is using language of consequence, because how writer talks to reader and how characters talk to each other depend on psychological circumstances.

Let's imagine a writer whose circumstances, from age eight to age twenty-four, lead her again and again to write stories whose style is either noncommittal or cynical. Jill is a twenty-four-year-old graduate student at a snappy writing workshop. She does not write beautiful literature. Jill is not a horrible person. Why is she deliberately writing ugliness?

I pretend I am a social worker and Jill has been sent to "see someone." She is a writer, and here is her story, the story of why Americans go out of their way to make ugly literature.

Jill was born in Lawrencetown, Massachusetts, the daughter of civilized parents who had stable notions and a safe house. She always wanted to be a writer.

She wrote her first official short story in the third grade. It was about the town dump, with its wheel spokes, bedsprings, moribund kittens in their gunny sack, rusting kitchen pots—all of which tell one another their stories. Dogs, cats, all domestic refugees come to the dump and tell all the ways they have been cruelly used. (Jill had imagination.) When she got her story back from the teacher, she found written on the bottom: "Jill, we have been studying sentences now for two years. You know perfectly well that a sentence begins with a capital letter and you need a period at the end."

What Jill learned from that comment was that psychological content in literature does not count. What counts is mechanics. Maybe that's right! her half-conscious mind says. After all, whenever you try to tell your stories at home, your mother says, "Boy, do kids have imagination!" to your dad. Both of them, mysteriously, in the next second, notice that you have tracked in mud, too.

When Jill was in fifth grade, she wrote another story for her English class. Unfortunately her school had not elected to get in a poet or storyteller from the Writers-in-the-Schools movement.[2] Her new story was about parents who were rude to their children—gratuitously rude. For interesting insights on parental rudeness to children, see Alice Miller's work, especially *For Your Own Good*.[3] Jill's parents were forever adjuring her to behave, but they were rude. This story came back with the comment that Jill's spelling was improved: the teacher had even drawn a smiling face at the bottom, with radiating lines coming out from it, indicating, I think, sunshine.

In the seventh grade, Jill happened to get an English teacher who herself did not read through any of the papers regarded as "creative writing" since creative writing was humanities fluff.

So Jill's third try at a story about rude parents was channelled like lock water into the peer-criticism pond. The peers, Jill's classmates, had now spent five years or more being told to respect mechanics more than content, mechanics more than content, mechanics more than content. It never crossed any of their minds to remark on anything more inner in Jill's work than her "effective sentences." If they had talked about Jill's content—the rudeness of her parents to her—it wouldn't have helped Jill much: empathy is ineffective between young peers. Its marvelous use for giving people confidence and verve works only when the empathizing is by an authority (parent or teacher or other wise adult)—not by other kids.

Jill did a well-imagined story in the tenth grade. Here is the plot: a tenth-grade girl came home from school to her parents' clean but uncultivated house in an industrial town near Andover, Massachusetts. The author tells us the house had wall-to-wall carpeting, which ran from the hallways into all the rooms, even her room. The previous owners had built a full-wall bookcase in the living room, but that didn't bother this girl's parents: they put their copy of *Reach Out* and their other book, *We Never Would Have Made It Without Him*, in the center of the eye-level shelf, and then placed glass bricks on both sides so the books stayed put. The girl threw one leg over the lounge-chair arm and listened to the baseboard heating for a while. Then she took down one of the books and studied the photo on the back jacket. It showed a woman sitting upright in a chair, and her husband sat on its arm, smiling. Both had excellent teeth. "Mom? Mom?" the girl said. Her mother appeared. "Mom, how much mousse do you suppose that lady's got on there to get that 360° look, anyhow?" The girl held up the book. "And those eyes, hey, Mom, like the dials on Dad's safe!" "Let me tell *you* something, young lady," the mother said, "before you make any more fun of those people of Jesus. You get this very straight. If we hear any more smart remarks from you about Jesus or the people of Jesus, your father will take it up with you. This is a Christ-centered home. You know what Christ-centered means? It means that if a certain young lady can't learn to love our Lord and Saviour, maybe she would like to just pick up and live somewhere else and see how *that* feels!"

Jill's teacher wrote on her story, "You don't give us any idea of the colors of the house. You say wall-to-wall carpeting, but we can't see it because we can't see the colors of it. You need to offer more physical description." She did not comment on the author's disdain for the religious parents and the Born-Again authors, nor on the mother's offering to throw the girl out if she couldn't get filled with the spirit. Religion is a chancy subject in American public schools, and, anyway, she had been teaching for twenty-four years and she knew her job: it was to tell Jill how *to polish her skills*, and *only* to polish her skills.

Jill read her comment. She felt the way you would if you went to a psychotherapist and cried, "I am in psychological pain!" and the therapist replied, "One thing sure—get that athlete's foot taken care of, pronto!"

Jill's parents' religion, and Jill's disdain for it, are *content*. By now, at sixteen, that part of Jill's personality which wants to feel disdain for parents and do either a little or a lot of "parent bashing" supposes that it can't be done in literature. That part of Jill balls itself up in its own fetal position, so to speak, and rolls away somewhere underneath the surface of Jill's mind, flattening other feelings as it goes. When you "negatively reinforce" one kind of expression in young people, you negatively reinforce several other kinds of expressiveness as well. We know that: look at the people who are "rigid and judgmental": it isn't just sensuality they can't praise; they find it very hard to praise anything. It is because the psychological muscle which praises got hurt some time in their past.

How one does a thing, Jill has now learned, *how* one does just the *surface* of it, is more important than *what* one does. She has learned that lesson three times over. She does not, therefore, major in English, as she once had wanted to. She majors in Business Administration, as do 25%–75% of undergraduates of small liberal-arts colleges and universities, who have been told that college is a tool for money-making, not learning for a good life.

Finally, the gorgeous day comes when she is relieved of college. She had a marvelous love affair, but college had been mostly boring.

After a year or two, Jill decides to try once more: she enters a graduate creative-writing workshop. She puts together a short fiction about two young adults who are fundamentalist in religion. They truck away all broken or dirty items from their house. They decide not to have a pet because you know pets. Jill, not skilled or disciplined enough to eschew Author Intrusions and Interior Monologue, tells us these two characters are vulgar, facile, evasive, and given to totalitarian ideas, although they talk about *koinonia* and *agape*. Jill gives us a sex scene. It is wretched sex.

Jill's teacher has, alas, seen so many such angry and stereotyping short stories that he is exasperated. He writes at the foot of the page, "You make your point all right, slam bang, but we can't get interested because we can't feel either love or pity for your characters."

This time Jill's development is not just balked: it is stunted. Likely Jill will now not become a writer, even a bad one. Jill's disgust for those characters was a genuine passion which in the course of twenty years she had nursed along under the surface. Her third-grade teacher discounted it without noticing it. Her tenth-grade teacher tried to distract her from it by asking, what color was the carpeting? instead of, what were some other meannesses about those parents? any kind things at all? Here then are the psychological suppressants which Jill has experienced so far:

1. No one who counts has "reflected back" Jill's fret about mean parents. She, therefore, thinks she was wrong to have such feelings. (This is a well-documented, very common response to psychological abuse of children.) Jill's disdain never gets refined.

2. Truth learnt in solitude and quiet insight itself apparently has no value: the only truth which gets respect appears to be what you learn from the powers that be.

3. Finally, Jill turns outward and asks, since my heart's truth apparently isn't much, what does count in literature? She sees our usual panoply—silvery little stories made up of shards of experience, quickly picked up, experienced by the reader the way a jogger sees the glitter of mica in clay. Well, that's one thing they want, Jill thinks, logically examining the technical surfaces of the stories she reads. Put it in the present tense, she thinks, to make *The New Yorker*. Have a misery going on under the surface without cure, but only small objects get discussed as properties of the drama—grass from the mower blade, oil spitting in a pan, congealed eggs on one's plate (that one's Hemingway's—a nice, miserable sort of parallel to the story content), and, of course, the crocodile of the American short story, narratives of male bonding through drinking and casual humping—done raucously by young writers, with nostalgia by the middle-aged, from habit and fear of change by the old.

The great stories are out there to be seen, too: Charles Baxter, Mark Helprin, Alice Munro, Margaret Atwood, Susan Lowell—but Jill's eyes are half-closed to them by now. There is a particular reason why she will not learn to write from these authors. She was never allowed to develop her own disdainful feelings, so she rolled them under. It means she never moved to the step which can follow disdain (in stage development): the stage of refining one's original feeling. Refining takes place only when a feeling has been heard by another human being:

Interviewer (or creative-writing teacher): "Jill, you show clearly about four or five ways in which your parents were cruel. Anything else?"

Jill: "What do you mean, anything else? Any other ways they were mean?"

Interviewer: "Yes—for starters. Yes. How else? Can you tuck anything else into this autobiographical piece of writing?"

Jill murmurs, "No—I think that's about it."

Interviewer (casually): "Well, anything else you want in here about the parents?" The interviewer is deliberately asking the question twice.

Jill: "They were great airplane-model-maker helpers. God, they were great. Hour after hour, Dad would hold the prop of the left engine of the P-38 while I wound up the starboard engine—you know, on a rubber band—then together we'd go out the door trying not to bang the plane. Mom rushed to the door and pulled the hydraulic stay-opener on the screen door, and Dad and I kind of shouldered each other out into the yard; Dad just got into the thing so goddamned well. 'This is M for Mongoose,' he would say, as we were hobbling to a good, open place to fly the plane. 'M for Mongoose, calling J for Jill, signal, J for Jill, when you are ready for take off.' He wouldn't be laughing either—looking fatherly. He would squint over the meadow, dead serious, with a perfect Southern accent like what you need for intercom talk in warplanes, dead serious, 'J for Jill, come in J for Jill, crissake come in, are you guys all right?' "

Interviewer: "Fantastic!"

Jill: "Well—yeah—yeah, so here's the thing—then he beat me up, because he said I closed my heart to Christ, you see, but when he was being the Control Tower, he was terrific."

Interviewer: "Complicated, you mean?"

Jill: "Both things going on in the same man at the same time."

Interviewer: "Listen, Jill—it's a wonderful, *wonderful*, complicated story. Think it through and do another draft. I'll read it. Just list everything about the man—don't say, he was this or he was that. A person is a lot of things. Also—just for fun—I want to see the P-38, too. If you get stuck, call. If you don't, good luck. See you Monday.''

If Jill had at any point in her writing participated in a conversation like this one, she would have learned you can talk frankly about evil, yet recognize that it sits next to good. She would have learned to see that one's first dash of judging human character is too simple: you can refine it.

But Jill is still left with a lot of unexpressed disdain.

Further, since she never got her disdain all written out, she will keep unconsciously circling round it. It will hide inside her, wrecking otherwise good, clean, new inspirations, wanting its way into her consciousness. It cries for attention, its *cris d'enfance* make such a racket inside her she doesn't hear happier voices, whose messages deserve at least as much attention.

When unconscious anger joins low self-esteem, an inexperienced author generally bends to write stories with jeering or chill feelings. The many American short stories in print which have low-life plots and obvious language work as role models for further cold-hearted narration. If one is, like the perfect C.I.A. recruit, "externalized," one will feel convinced that flip or chill writing is *de rigueur* in the short story.

Jill wrote a story in which a couple drink and carp at one another in a dumpyard, although Jill herself was having a gorgeous love affair with a fellow grad student named Henry. She and Henry spent some of their time on stepladders in the back aisles of Barnes & Noble, looking at photographs of our planet in a geology text or two. In one text, Figure 24 showed a pen-and-ink-drawn section of our world's crust. Some of the flat, generally horizontal strata were filled with regularly placed plus-signs, looking for all the world like a military graveyard. Other layers were filled with dozens of regularly placed hyphens. There were wonderful words in the captions: *extrusions, lobes, dolomite*. On the right-hand page, Figure 25 was a b/w photograph of flat land strewn with greenstone and some peaked-looking little lakes: Northern Minnesota, the caption explained, abraded by glaciers—and under its chill and scarified flesh, rockmolt still shoving about, meeting lenient or stubborn strata. All that lay under Henry's and Jill's feet: the cheerful moral of that story is that little of what counts makes it to the surface. The passers-by in Barnes & Noble got no glimpse of Jill's and Henry's caring: they were so close to one another they felt as if all the geomorphology of twelve thousand years (at least what they knew of it from Figures 24 and 25!) were part of their life together.

If Jill's own young-adult life was so pleasant, why did she choose to write a story about a night watchman for an old people's home who made out with his girl in the gravel pit and later crept into the Home residents' rooms to steal? Why would Jill choose savagery for her subject?

We have seen how various teachers blocked her from handling the cruelties she observed. Further, she came, let's say, from a nonliterary family. Jill's family thought of reading as something you do to find out what's rotten going on somewhere, the way one reads a newspaper. Most people who don't read serious literature suppose that literature is exposé. Their mindset when reading or writing is to expose some evil or other. This is the mindset of junior high-schoolers, too: all their lives they haven't been allowed to talk back to parents. Then they get a creative-writing assignment: it's the first chance of their lifetimes to conduct some parent bashing without reprisal.

Ugly Facts of Our Time and Our Sense of the Public Concern

Because our Jill's and other jacks' and jills' work is ugly, journal- and diary-writers hunch their shoulders against it. Alas, this wraps them further in their own lives and delays their taking on some care for the *res publica*. This just when the world desperately needs public-minded literature. Here is Tom Wolfe arguing for literature taking on the public issues:

> Young writers are constantly told, "Write about what you know." There is nothing wrong with that rule as a starting point, but it seems to get quickly magnified into an unspoken maxim:

The only valid experience is personal experience . . . Dickens, Dostoyevsky, Balzac, Zola, and Sinclair Lewis assumed that the novelist had to go beyond his personal experience and head out into society as a reporter.[4]

Christa Wolf (in *Accident/A Day's News*) recognizes how much anyone wants not to worry over the public world. People "want to sit back in their armchairs after a hard day's work like me and have their beer—wine in my case, what of it—and they want to be presented (on TV) with something that makes them happy, a complicated murder plot, for example, but nothing which affects them too much and that is the normal behavior we have been taught so that it would be unjust to reproach them for this behavior merely because it contributes to our deaths."[5] Morally speaking, that is one of the fastest-moving long sentences I've read! It explains why for every Susan Lowell who makes herself focus on how the United States irradiated an entire family in her story "White Canyon,"[6] there are thousands of writers who practice what therapists call "pain avoidance." Crimes by government and scientists are so painful to think of, most writers, most readers, stay clear of them.

One cure for Jill, even for many Jills, is to remember that at any one time there are at least two injustices being perpetrated somewhere. Such awareness gives you perspective without making you shrill: the two injustices can be far off. Tolstoy's greatest gift to modern literature is moral scope. The notion is this: while you are absorbed in your provincial affairs, elsewhere some evil is being forwarded by courteous people who belong to a financially powerful group. While you are fixing a man's buttonhole so he and his friend may stand together at his marriage, you see from the vestry window someone hunting deeply in the garbage can across the street. Tolstoy always brought in such perspective:

During an interval in the Melvinski trial, in the large building of the Law Courts, the members and the public prosecutor met . . . while Peter Ivanovich, not having entered into the discussion at the start, took no part in it but looked through the

Gazette which had just been handed in. "Gentleman," he said, "Ivan Ilyich has died!"[7]

Since Tolstoy knows we all live our lives in the shadow of laws, governments, either inside or outside the right clubs, he bothers to mention such things. We know from the paragraph above that he will tell us a story in which justice, law, establishment, and death will each share some time onstage. Once we know that our hobbies and love affairs and job hunting and funeral arrangements are all going to take place in a world which also has governments and corporations, we mustn't pretend otherwise—not if we're serious. As Christa Wolf says, "We have pushed off from the animal kingdom for good."[8]

We can do any number of grimy narratives like those Jill feels driven to write, and still turn them into beautiful literature by *giving them their full setting*. If the *major considerations* are present in a work, then some low-intensity realism can come in without foundering the whole piece. Even such a disdainful passage as the one below, in which the author looks down on the protagonist, can take place in a short story provided the general scope is big enough:

> He told me to take them back before I'd lose the papers. Now, Sears will let you exchange, all right, without you got the papers, but they do always ask you to have the papers when you exchange, if you can remember. God, when I think of the number of times I've brought back stuff to Sears! Things I bought in good faith, or worse, his things! Machinery, workgloves, cloth, tools—things in the catalogue he thought he wanted and no sooner do I get home from picking them up then he wants me to take them back and exchange them!

The paragraph shows us a workingman's wife expressing irritation: because we see her focus on minutia, we take her for not only tiresome or ill-tempered, but petty as well. A whole short story about her and the people she consorts with might well end up a peevish tale without a sympathetic protagonist.

Yet all one has to do to make the dullest people sympathetic is set them in their periphery. There are two psychological reasons for that: first, as every intervention con-sultant knows, to get some level of a) tolerance and then b) understanding going between people or between a person's idea of self and the real self, you widen the conversation to include as much of the person's anecdotes as you can. As the circle of events in that person's life is mentioned, widening, including more events, the way the wave goes outward from the stone thrown in the pond, some of the events mentioned will be of universal interest. At some point, since we live in a finite world, one comes across things which the more boring people have in common with the most interesting people. Spouses of diplomats are constantly forced to have superficial, cordial conversations. If they have been diplomats' spouses long enough, they know how to race through the "And how is the family?" punctilio as fast as they can and get to a shared hobby. The same thing works in fiction. In the passage on the next page, the hobbies are used-car-lot dealing, boring support groups, and getting drunk.

The second psychological reason for setting people in the widest possible periphery of their lives is that it increases our affection for them. Human beings are rather too much like the watchdogs Plato talked about in Book II of *The Republic*: we don't like what we don't know (two-year-old children loathe mayonnaise because they have never tasted it) and we do like—just as inappropriately—what we do know. The most astounding case of this I ever knew of had to do with a high-school teacher who threw pencils at the students in his French class. I heard about it and called the principal to ask if he was firing the French teacher. Well, no, I guess not, the principal said, because if we fire him, we'd have to hire someone else, and while he isn't the greatest, at least we know him, and if we hire someone new, he'd be an unknown factor.

It is easy to jeer at such a stupid allowance made to a bully, but a grimmer look at the same mindset reminds us of the hundreds and thousands of human beings who have been equable about child labor

slavery

sadistic behavior of males to females

the disparity between rich people's fun and
poor people's desperation

only because those evils are familiar. Familiarity may occasionally breed the contempt Bolingbroke spoke of: most of the
time it breeds what John Kenneth Galbraith called "accommodation" to injustice.

In literature, telling the whole story about some deplor-
able person or situation breeds a good kind of accommodation
in both reader and author. The more we know about a character, the more like one of us the character appears. Jill, the
young writer with the poor creative-writing background, could
exchange her over-all cynicism for a combination of general
affection and specific wrath if she would drop the practice of
minimalism. When she writes her dumpyard relationship as a
minimalist narrative, she starts with disaffection and ends with
disaffection. If she pulled in all kinds of peripheral life for the
dumpyard couple, she could still do a story disdaining their
inchoate relationship, but the moral tone would brighten.

Here is an example of how a grungy passage can change
into a human predicament worth bothering putting into story,
just by the author's listing more about the person. First, she
needs a name: it will be Kate.

> Kate got disgusted with Donny about the Sears purchases.
> Donny beat her some. She guessed she was a battered wife.
> Their town was beautiful. Halfway between St. Fursey Lake,
> Minnesota, and St. Paul.
>
> She liked getting juiced with Donny. She didn't see him as
> your average wife-beater. She saw him as someone who can't
> read a Sears catalogue with enough imagination to know if he
> wants something or what.
>
> This one time she got to meet what she guessed was a real
> idealist. Some guy had lost his job because he refused to work

on chemical warfare. His buddy explained to Kate he was a whistleblower. Kate had never met any of those types before.

Then the whistle-biower's buddy slugged Donny right there in the booth.

Once Kate talked Donny into letting her keep a kitten she and their daughter found at the dump.

Their daughter got in trouble, but that was a lot later.

Every so often, Donny did something so charming and funny, she would decide he was a wonderful man and she was crazy to listen to those support-group women talking about shelters. The funniest time was when he took her and their daughter to the used-car dealer in St. Fursey and said "Here we go, girls! Here we go! Don't talk, either of you! Don't show you like a car; let me do the talking." Then he and the dealer gave them rides in various Honda Civic Wagons, of '84, '85, '86, and '87, the years Donny was interested in. Donny made a lot of jokes. Usually the dealer could see the joke, too. Sometimes the jokes seemed mean at first, but everyone laughed and you got to have fun. "She don't say nothing," Donny would laugh, jerking his head over towards Kate. "Can't tell if you like the car." Kate giggled. Or Donny would say, "Well, old lady, what do you think?" and the dealer would smile at Kate but she kept her mouth shut good and Donny turned to the dealer. "No deal," Donny would say, "She don't like it." This went on for an hour and a half anyway. Finally Donny got $850 off an '84 and a real tire thrown in instead of that shrinkeroo spare the car came with . . . It takes a man.

The leader of Kate's support group didn't know how to tell her she was boring the group, taking up too much air time.

Donny said as long as that kitten grew up male, o.k., but if it was female it had to go to Doc Buchwald and that was the end of it.

Kate once met a real whistle-blower whose friend slugged her husband in the face and Donny never broke her jaw again.

I like Kate better now. Her style is still U.S.A.-Casual, and what's more, she not only is peevish about minutia, as we knew from the Sears passage, but she likes being drunk and she bores her support group. But now we know three universal and not despicable qualities in her: first, she has met and taken cognizance of a whistle-blower. She therefore joins, however tangentially, the world of shall-we-or-shall-we-not-do-evil-work-for-our-boss. Second, Kate shares at least one major value with the former First Lady of the United States. Like Mrs. Bush, Kate "would regret time not spent with a husband, a child, a friend, or a parent." She would more than agree with Mrs. Bush's warning not "to lose the most important investment you will ever make." (All over the world, of course, there are social workers and psychotherapists who wish that the concept of husband-as-investment would not reach the ears of battered women: fear of losing that investment is one of the powerful forces which keeps battered women battered.) Leaving aside how inappropriately Kate would apply Mrs. Bush's strictures to her own life, we have at least got our female protagonist linked to a decent, major idea. And finally, Kate has a decent, major emotion as well: she is capable of simple, cheerful admiration, whether or not Donny's aplomb in the used-car lot deserves it.

America has a good deal of ugly-hearted fiction. Some of the violence in it is salacious: that is, the author gets a kick out of thinking about it and knows the reader will, too. But some is a mistake in calculation: the author thinks that exposing the reader to this or that specific grunge or evil will teach the reader not to participate in that grunge or evil. In fact, people imitate what they see most sensually put before them—rather than learning from the moral brought out at the end of anything. We know this from television: people are imitating the violence they see, quarter-hour by quarter-hour; the police dramas do not teach them that crime doesn't pay, no matter how many last thirty seconds are given to showing the criminals being caught. In literature, shabby emotions or evil emotions inform the work if they take up all its pages. There will always be salacious writers. Let's set their work aside. Our question is: how can anxious Americans put evil or dingy situations into short stories without rotting the tone? I think Tolstoy's method is best: put in so much else of the characters' lives that the periphery of their worlds overlaps the periphery of all our worlds. Chapters 3, 7, and 8 take up ways to work such perspective into short stories.

INTRODUCTION: NOTES

1. Charles Baxter, "Scheherazade," *Harper's,* June 1989.

2. Writers-in-the-Schools Program, founded by COMPAS, the St. Paul, Minnesota-based arts organization.

3. Alice Miller, *For Your Own Good: Hidden Cruelty in Child-Rearing and the Roots of Violence,* translated by Hildegarde & Hunter Hannum, Farrar, Straus & Giroux, New York, 1983. Early works by Alice Miller: *Prisoners of Childhood* (reissued in paperback as *The Drama of the Gifted Child*), *Thou Shalt Not Be Aware: Societies' Betrayal of the Child,* and *Pictures of a Childhood: 66 Watercolors and an Essay.*

4. Tom Wolfe, "Stalking the Billion-Footed Beast: A Literary Manifesto, for the New Social Novel," *Harper's,* November 1989, p. 45.

5. Christa Wolf, *Accident/A Day's News,* translated by Heike Schwarzbauer & Rick Takvorian, Farrar, Straus & Giroux, New York, 1989.

6. Susan Lowell, *Ganado Red,* Milkweed Editions, Minneapolis, 1989. Also of interest, the *New York Times,* June 7, 1990, reports that the House of Representatives has approved a bill to give financial compensation and a government apology to uranium miners and to people downwind of the Nevada Nuclear Testing Site who now suffer from radiation sickness. The *Times* reports: "From 1945 to 1963, the Federal Government tested atomic weapons in the atmosphere, exposing about 220,000 military personnel and 150,000 civilians to radiation."

7. Leo Tolstoy, "The Death of Ivan Ilyich," translated by Louise and Aylmer Maude, *Fiction 100: An Anthology of Short Stories,* 4th edition, ed. James H. Pickering, Macmillan, New York, 1985, p. 1034.

8. Christa Wolf, *Accident/A Day's News,* p. 90.

Making Your Heart's Truth into Literature

The Passionate, Accurate Story

First Draft Work Is Like No Other Work in the Story

The Approach of Critics Is Not the Approach of Writers

Many of the ideas of literary critics are recklessly carried over into the field of writing literature. Criticism is analysis: it is breaking down an already-made thing into its components so one can see those components. It does not help makers of things to do analysis at the time they are doing the making. Making is putting together components which look pretty disparate: writers, in fact, deliberately have to prevent themselves from analyzing too soon what they've put down on paper: the disparate components will still look too unpromising. Writers work as much on hope and hunch as on logic. (Psychological logic has its uses—but they come in later.)

The more original a short-story writer, the odder looking the assortment of things he or she puts together for a story. Jules-Henri Poincaré said the same of scientists: a dull one builds theories on phenomena close at hand and of an apparently germane kind. An imaginative scientist sees connections between phenomena which may stand both physically and associatively at great distance from one another. The last thing in the world either author or scientist—or indeed, any kind of a brainstormer—should do is assess components too early.

It is natural to trust literary analysis. Our dreadful obsession with technique has been with us since

18

junior-high-school English classes. Those paragraphs—study questions, or whatever they are called—at the ends of stories and poems in our junior- and senior-high-school anthologies are the anthrax of literary criticism: "What techniques did the author use to gain such and such an effect?" "How did the author deploy his characters?" "Why does the author say such and such in the third paragraph: how does that affect the tone? the theme?" "What strategies did the author, etc., etc." We know that young Americans who as children liked reading grow to hate their junior-high-school English classes. No wonder. A parallel in religion would be: if one has ever loved God, one would hate hours of contemplating how the liturgy of the third and fourth centuries A.D. evolved to accommodate Roman bureaucratic structures. No one enjoys losing passionate content to technique. Why wreck personal enjoyment?

More importantly: inventions, like scientific discoveries, do not start with a listing of components—conflict, tone, characters, theme, beginning, middle, ending, etc. Inventions come from one's original ideal joined with whatever service the imagination subsequently offers. For a short-story writer, a story is a combination of what the writer *supposed* the story would likely be about—plus what actually turned up in the course of writing. For this kind of process, literary criticism is of no use at all.

At no point in his writing of "The Rocking-Horse Winner" would it have helped D.H. Lawrence to be told, "You're doing a short story? Oh, then! You must have a beginning, a middle, and an end! And you must have conflict! And tone! And mind the *unity:* if you are doing a story about parental failings, you had better think twice before putting in the supernatural!" Lawrence's genius was that he ever even thought of using the supernatural alongside all else in that story—the wonderfully grim mother, the dining room with its flowers out of season, the game little gardener with his bets, the uncle with *his* bets, the excitement of the Lincoln, the Ascot, the old tried-and-true addiction of Englishmen—sending one's kid to Eton.

The First Draft

We have to approach the first draft of a short story entirely differently from how we work on any of the subsequent drafts. This is the draft in which we do no assessing and no organizing because we are inventing. We are still generating, not judging. In the first draft, we get to be like people in journal courses: we simply write.

It is difficult to understand why anyone should mindlessly *write* when so many experts have taught us so many techniques for smartening up short stories. It all has to do with the idea that the short story is made of two psychological elements: the story we set down to work on, and the mysterious additions which will join that story (radically change it, as often as not). These mysterious additions will join *only* if the author writes without any harassment by the critical faculty. We must waive all memories of discussions of authors' techniques. (It would be a tremendous help if high-school texts carried *no* discussions of authors' techniques in their otherwise excellent anthologies of stories and poems. Instead, there could be Study Questions about the authors' insights on life.)

It is hard to stem the technique-loving tide in our minds—even long enough to write an ambling first draft. Technique has a charismatic pull, a pull felt at least as strongly by mediocre minds as by imaginative ones. People love to ruminate over *how* to pull something off. They understand artists or scientists or philosophers as technicians of some high order. Tolstoy has a passage about just this. It is the scene in *Anna Karenina* in which Vronsky and Anna visit a painter named Mihailov. They have come to see his painting, *Christ before Pilate*. Some comments float about the studio, and then Vronsky says, turning to one of his party, "How those figures in the background stand out! There's technique for you." Tolstoy tells us that "this remark about technique jarred painfully on Mihailov, and he gave Vronsky an angry look. He was always hearing that word technique, and could never make out what people understood by it."

The angry look which Mihailov so understandably gave

Vronsky is the angry look which Jill must have wanted to give, in turn, to her third-grade, fifth-grade, seventh-grade, and tenth-grade English teachers. With despatch, then, I'd like to list three common *bêtes noires* which teachers and critics wish upon fiction writers. All three are not only useless but they hobble short-story plot from the free flight it wants.

1. No story we mean to write has a Beginning, a Middle, or an Ending. As Lewis Thomas says in *The Lives of a Cell: Notes of a Biology Watcher*, we do most of our basic research in a spirit of hope and humor and likely failure. All first drafts of all stories are basic research: the ending is not yet known. We *suspect* something telling lies ahead.

2. It is no good being told: "Get conflict in it." It is not only no good, however: it is bad. Conflict implies an abutment of two people or two issues, when a first-rate story ought to handle many. Very little that is interesting in life comes in poles—this versus that. Students cling to the "story must have a conflict" theory, of course. They need to think how that idea of conflict suggests two subjects, when at least three keep appearing in any lifelike case. For example, in André Dubus's "A Father's Story,"[1] a father covers up the manslaughter which his daughter commits through drunken driving. If we consider the plot as conflict, we'd be likely to write off some of the real, ethical content; we would take the conflict to be whether or not he should have covered up for her murder. It makes a partial issue (the cover-up) seem like the whole content. Subtler aspects of that story are the narrator's relations with Roman Catholic authority, and both the father's and daughter's indifference to the dead man's surviving family.

3. Writers should eschew the language of war unless they are fond of killing eighteen-through-thirty-five-year-olds and long for the battlefield. The metaphors we use role model certain values. Metaphors create norms. Therefore, words never to be used about short-story writing are "conflict," "strategies

for writing," "attacking" the subject, "getting a line" on a character, "hitting the mark," "making a straight shot." George Orwell has pointed out that not only do shoddy cultures produce shoddy language, but shoddy language in its turn produces still more shoddy culture. It is the same with hostile language: it reinforces hostile instincts.

I was interested in Janet Burroway's saying that "A story is a war."[2] Her book, *Writing Fiction*, is one of the most thoroughgoing and useful manuals I have seen, but there is that odd philosophy. I have decided we have so much war language in our culture, that even highly civilized people use war metaphors without noticing. Because they do not attach importance to such usage does not make it good: unconsciousness of evil does not obliterate the evil. Genet's play, *The Screens*, is extraordinarily cruel, even for Genet. The actors insult the audience directly (as is common in Genet), but hundreds of people in an audience I was part of didn't *feel themselves insulted*. They decided that Genet "is just that way." He is, of course. Like battering husbands and like middle-aged men who plan wars. I think it is important to be conscious of such language.

There are thousands of American writers taking M.F.A.s in creative writing. If all those thousands become accustomed and thus numbed to the use of war metaphors, we have a psychological and ethical risk. I offer the suggestion that we pretend that short-story writing has an ethics code in the way that other informal professions have scruples and standards.

Leaving the *Donnée*: Inviting the Unconscious

Just as literary criticism has for one of its aims *seeing through* the literature-under-discussion, writers need to get a little lost in the literature-about-to-be. What is a short story as seen by someone still writing it? It is the *first element*, the story we consciously intend to write, and then it is at least a second, if not third, element given us as we are writing along. It is useful to have this firm definition: it stops the scalding conversations about agreeing on a definition. People are forever announcing that something can't be defined, when nearly everything can be defined so long as you are willing to be mistaken.

For example, what is an essay? An essay is a work of literary art which has a minimum of one anecdote and one universal idea. If it has no anecdote, it is at best doctrine and at worst shouting in the motel bar. If it has no universal idea, and its anecdote is autobiographical, it is at best autobiography, at worst shouting in the motel bar. If it has no idea and its anecdote is not autobiographical but is true of someone else, it is at best biography or history, and at worst gossip. In any case, it is an essay as soon as it has *both* idea and true anecdote. And it is 3000% easier to write than a short story.

A writer experiences a short story as joining the two elements I mentioned: the conscious start-up element—and then the mysterious second aspect which joins on, like someone joining a train when it makes a dark night stop. Henry James made up the expression *donnée*, French for "given"— meaning what is given at the start. James, who irritated a good many people a good deal of the time, was especially irritating at dinner parties where he occasionally interrupted someone who was telling an anecdote: "Wait! Stop!" James would cry in more or less these words: "I've got it. . . . " What he meant was he had taken your anecdote mid telling and had seen how he might attach it to some mysterious second element which *he* would find or devise, and then make a perfect short story. Infuriating, of course. Your whole dinner-party joke was just lighter fluid to James.

The luck or genius in a short-story writer comes to bear when he or she leaps off the lily pad of the *donnée*, inspired by moral indignation or joy or general affection or a fit of laughter, and flings the writing towards the invisible *second element*. . . . Think how many times D.H. Lawrence must have heard Lincoln- and Ascot-related conversations in his lifetime before he thought to use material about horse racing in connection with empty-hearted parents!

Apropos of Lawrence, here is psychological advice to writers: make a short list of those authors whose work seems magical to you. (My list would include D.H. Lawrence, Leo Tolstoy, the Virginia Woolf of *The Three Guineas*, the Mark Helprin of "The Schreuderspitze."[3]) Then, looking over the list, tell yourself how despicably unfair it is that these people are inventive, so morally lively, so lithe at phrase, so full of particular and beautiful memories. The whole world is unfair and always has been, tell yourself aloud. Next, having said all that (for you are right: it *is* unfair), don't ever pine to be like those writers again. Only do your work. If you find yourself pining, have the list out again. Scold the world for its unfairness again and then drop it again. The pain of lesser imagination is genuine enough; Dylan Thomas bows to it when he talks of "wise men whose words have forked no lightning" feeling balked.[4] It is hard to describe oneself as someone of lesser gift, but it is invaluable to do so for about one split second only. (For more in the same vein, please see pp. 102-103.)

Leaving the *donnée* is the literary step which divides journal-writers and autobiographers from short-story writers. It is a fierce discipline. It is leaving behind the way things happened in your own life, leaving behind what actually happened which you are dying to (as they say) "capture." Literature is not about capturing anything: it is about a mysterious marriage of what really happened (the *donnée*) and how your mind organizes it together with feeling and unknown things. The unknown things—which I call "the second element"—of a short story can't be known until you have made up your mind to leave the *donnée*.

Here is the psychological stamina it takes: detachment from self, loss of self, faith that external life is not nearly so interesting as internal, sensual, moral life. A good short story is nearly never about "what actually happened." It is at least half about humanity and our earth. That is why writing teachers sigh when a student-writer cries, "O but that's what actually happened!" What actually happened is only grist or start-up. The teacher sighs because the student still clings to it. It is very difficult to teach navigation theory to someone who clings to the shore.

In the 1990s, there are so many people writing journals and even taking courses in writing journals that the distinction between journal and story is weakening. Unfortunately, there are dozens of teachers of journalistic or memoir writing for every theorist about short-story writing. All sorts of people help both young and old to write down their experiences. It is a marvelous bright corner of our cultural life. What's more, most of the old bad elementary and junior-high-school teachers are by now either shamed or retired, so children are no longer told writing is only for a few. But our anti-intellectual culture still generally jeers at people who are contemplative. Nietzsche tells us that uncultivated people really hate cultivated people. Some of the elementary-school teachers in a project called "Growing Up American"[5] at the College of St. Scholastica, in Duluth, summer of 1989, admitted to not having really seen the point of literature before they joined the project. A few mentioned having an actual aversion to literature.

Psychology examines such aversion or even hatred and shows us ways to change it. Specifically, psychotherapy is oddly useful to writers. Clients, like writers, have to leave behind their autobiographical *données*. The *donnée*, as therapists know, is external. What a client—or story writer—needs to become is inward.

Here is the crux of it: between the conscious and unconscious mind we are more complex and given to concept than we are just in the conscious mind. This means we must somehow get more use out of the unconscious part. But the unconscious has no idea of being dutiful. To waken it, we try laying some sensual or aesthetic or moral excitement just under its nose: the fragrance will rouse it from its torpor, we hope. The unconscious mind had much rather remain sleeping, of course: it knows what it's doing. If it wanted to be awake all the time, it would be the conscious mind. It is powerful: it holds most of our memories. It has a penchant for terror and for self-defense. If not tempted by other nourishment, it will content itself with lurching to its feet just when we don't want it to, attacking someone senselessly. It is as much soup as animal. It prefers steeping away to thinking. It is a mess, but in its mess lie impressions life once gave us. We want them to freight our hearts' truths in short stories.

Psychotherapists know that if a client or patient says aloud the facile ideas he or she has absorbed from around town or from parents or from idle thinking, more specific, more accurate assessments may percolate upward from underneath. You can imagine a human head: draw a horizontal line from the eyebrow line to the back: above this line are the shallow ideas we and our neighbors, lightweight journalists and just anyone with authority or a big mouth, pass around back and forth like sea foam on the tide. When any of that material is *expressed to a serious hearer*—or seriously written down and read by an adult reader, the mind changes. Unconscious fragments run upward to fill the vacuum left by the exiting clichés, the way bright magma comes licking upward in the cracks when the earth's crust shifts.

Here is another picture: we pretend that the unconscious itself is a psychological client on its own. It needs a hearer. It wants to know someone for the moment. U.C. (Unconscious Mind) is delighted to see that the C.M. (Conscious Mind) is going to a serious writing class. The owner (the whole person, that is) is lifting the weight of stale ideas and images off its head. There is space up there! Well, U.C. says, in its scattered, poorly enunciated way (since it never knows the end or the beginning of any conversation, it never has any particular purposes), "Well, I see what's going on here! My person has got rid of that obvious stuff! It's finally *gone*! Well, then! Since the owner is serious about writing things down, I will keep filling that upper mental space with more subtle, more daring, weirder connections than C.M. ever dreamed of!"

This new unconscious material never would have begun its drift to the surface unless the owner had written the *donnée*. Please know: a short story must have its *donnée* before any *second element* will join. A short story cannot be planned ahead. O we make the plans!—but they are plans like Levin's hunting with his dog Laska, in *Anna Karenina*. Levin directed Laska to nose here and there, in the slough: a conscious, planning, bureaucratic sort of hunter, Levin directed everything. All the while his dog pretended to obey him, but the true scent drew her in other directions. She pretended to hunt where Levin sent her, she wagged her tail to show how much she loved him, but she drew him to the prey elsewhere, despite his resistance. Because we cannot know the true plot of a story until we have written quite a lot of it, I use the vague expression "second element."

Writers and literary teachers have said one thing or another about how subsequent drafts of stories bring in subtler material, but psychotherapists are explicit. (If people of another discipline can help us write imaginatively, let's not hesitate to use their wisdom any longer than if we were used to reading by candlelight, we would hesitate to get in electric lights.) When you jump the ship of your familiar, conscious ideas, the therapists tell us, you change.

There are immediate rewards to letting a first draft maunder about in whatever direction it seems to want. For one thing, a predetermined plot tends to bear false or incomplete witness: we get our minds set on the beginning, the development, and the ending, and then drive through to that particular ending even if the rough manuscript itself keeps shouting, That isn't how those people would really feel! Predetermined outcomes in the short-story plot are like topical research in science: they leave no room for discovery. They prevent one's following surprise tendrils of interest.

Here is an example of a scene in which, let us say, we have decided we want to have a woman named LaVonne and a man named Vern court and then marry.

> It is 1978. Vern has a small sailboat on a northern lake. He loves to tighten sheet: the deck takes its cant, LaVonne sits in the bow so she needn't bend over when he brings the boat about. Her hair (of course) blows backward, and it is clean.

> They have landed on a wooded island and are eating. Then they make love, only very slightly S&M love in the sense that LaVonne tells him "You were wonderful" instead of "We were wonderful."

Now we decide we would like an image. Something for them to talk about before they agree to marry.

"I love sailing," Vern says lazily. His arm is around her shoulders, and her hair (the same hair that blew back from her seat forward of the mast) has fallen, beautifully fallen onto his arm and shoulder.

LaVonne says, "Yeah, it's O.K., sailing, I mean. But of course there's nothing like a really sharp inboard!"

Maugham would no sooner have seen LaVonne and Vern landing on that beach than he would have asked, "What about the American class system?" LaVonne's speech brings it in: if this is a first draft and we are flexible, we see that LaVonne and Vern may marry but there will be serious griefs. If we fail to see that our own unconscious mind brought LaVonne's remark into the draft, if we drive through to the end with our original idea, we will have to amend LaVonne's remark, pretend it didn't happen—simply carry on. Stories planned for a market generally do just that, of course. It is their characteristic way of skewing their author's real truths.

It is a waste not to stand back a little from the first draft: how the first draft lists will show us how the story should blow.

The most common form of conscious-mind-only writing is writing for a market. Directing one's plot to suit a predetermined audience is like going to a psychotherapist to learn some truth, then going home and asking relations, neighbors, and clergy people what they think, and deciding in favor of their collective wisdom. Peter Elbow wrote a marvelous essay, "Closing My Eyes as I Speak: An Argument for Ignoring Audience,"[6] in which he gave the morally sophisticated reasons for ignoring audience. He takes a firm stance against the usual counsel to writing students. As soon as you hear, "You must think about whom you're writing for," you need to realize you are talking to a market-driven person, not someone interested in the *basic research* which at least that part of literature we call the first draft must be.

It is very hard to leave one's *donnée*. If one is content with one's vivid autobiographical descriptions or reflections, one is not likely to long for the scudding fragmented weather of *other*.

The moral philosopher and developmental educator Lawrence Kohlberg inquired into how people get helped or blocked from ascending the stages of cognitive and moral development.[7] He noted that children growing up in homes and communities where abstract ideas are talked about move from concrete self-absorption more quickly than children from homes or communities where the conversations are mainly anecdotes. Since anecdotes, mindless anecdotes, probably make up 97% of the world's human conversations, it is amazing anyone moves into genuine intellectual life! Middle-class children, Kohlberg found, move up through cognitive stages more quickly than the children of uneducated parents, partly because they hear abstract concepts talked about. They are exposed to reflective thinking and symbolization. Kohlberg was not an elitist: in fact, his use of stage-development theory is freeing: it says that we all have a chance to move from stage to stage; it says that some cultural environments are especially encouraging to cognitive and moral growth. That's cheerful news: it means, all we have to do is give children an environment friendly to reflective thinking. Or at the least, see if we can intervene where children are exposed to environments which stunt curiosity, delight, and imagination. Here is an example of an environment specifically friendly to literary thinking.

> Natalie said at supper, "Mom. Dad. You know the house next door with the Merrill Lynch sign up?"
> "Has someone bought that?" asked the mother.
> Natalie: "Today I think a small family of bears has moved in there, what looks like the mom, dad or uncle, and cub."
> Natalie's dad: "How'd you get onto that? Did you see them taking the garbage out? It's Tuesday—that's garbage day, well, for humans it is, anyhow."
> Natalie: "Not just the garbage, Dad. One hundred containers of Quaker Rolled Oats on the sidewalk."
> Mother: "If you're right, Nat, I'm going over with a hot dish. Neighbors did that for us when *we* moved in."

The above story-sharing says to Natalie that imagination is adventure, a form of love. But here is the far more common course such a conversation would take:

Natalie at supper, "Mom. Dad. You know the house next door with the Merrill Lynch sign up?"

"Has someone bought that?" asked the mother.

Natalie: "Today I think a small family of bears has moved in there, what looks like the mom, dad or uncle, and cub."

Dad: "Talk about *imagination*!"

The down-putting in the second example is mild. Its message, however, is that imagination should be outgrown and delight is not an emotion. By the time most children are seven or eight years old, their storytelling instinct is damped down. Further, once in the third grade, they are likely to get a teacher who will indicate very clearly that writing is a question of mechanical proficiency.

Leaving the *Donnée* as a Form of Love of the Universe

For the moment, let's make a mental image of people who kid. Kidding is low-level jeering done with a small smile as you speak. To kid people skillfully:

1. Regard their imaginative impulse and philosophical remarks as absurd.

2. Note that you are either legion (like peers in school) or powerful (like a parent), so don't hesitate. Move forward and kid.

3. Note that you can serve two masters at once here: you can have the pleasure of putting down this person at the same time as you smile to show that he or she would be a poor sport to take your kidding amiss. If the smile doesn't work, if the victim doesn't look crestfallen-but-game, like a hazed first-year cadet at Annapolis, you can follow up with, "Can't take kidding?" If even that doesn't work to generate just the satisfying mix of shame and passivity which bullies enjoy in a child's

face, you can add, "I'll tell you one thing: you're not going to get very far in this world without a sense of humor."

The conversation above is straight grunge: no one in Jane Austen's novels would speak to someone else like that, but in the United States most citizens don't believe in psychological awareness, so without even noticing, they conduct cruel conversations. They develop a few sadistic routines. These routines give a little pleasure and don't seem to do any harm at the moment. If no one has read *The Three Guineas* or anything like it, if no one has read *The Abolition of Man*,[8] or anything like it—if no one is conscious of stunting young people's joy in life, then that family goes ahead and kids the child. Besides, it's been a bad day, it's hard to make a living. Sometimes kids just hang around until you're ready to go straight up the wall, and then some dumb remark gets made at supper about bears moving into a vacant house, so what the hell? Ernest Becker points out something to our purpose here: he says that upper-class people who are depressed because they are experiencing *meaning-loss* feel guilty: they feel that because they are privileged, they ought to be grateful and happy. Lower-class people, however, don't think they ought to be happy. When they experience depression, they don't fall into self-accusation: they call out their scapegoats instead:

> On the other hand, among the lower classes, dissatisfaction need not necessarily terminate in depressive self-accusation. Any number of scapegoats can be found and other rationalizations used, to justify failure: the rich, the boss, the low status of women in the lower class *as compared with* the upper, "bad luck," "hard times," and so on.[9]

Suppose we say to Natalie's parents in the instance of the conversation about the bears next door: "Might you, for the sake of your daughter's imaginative development, sacrifice the small pleasure of jeering at her and regarding her imaginative remarks as 'the dumb kind of stuff kids say at supper?' "

The idea of an environment (the home) as being encouraging or not encouraging to development of the imagination is not a widespread or even recognized interest of most human beings. For every parent who knows that children's books need to be stories, not facts prettily presented, there are likely tens of thousands who have never turned over in their minds the idea that *being able to make a hypothesis* is one of the key functions of the human intellect. We are a creature that learns by making a scenario of likely outcomes, should we take such and such an action. Once anyone has learned to enjoy making scenario—doing geometric hypotheses, telling the ends of stories begun somewhere else—it is a pleasure never dropped.

This is a privileged secret, however. Surely Natalie's parents have never been told about psychological advantage or psychological stunting. It is a ghastly injustice that children read aloud to are invited into the joy of imagination and children not read aloud to are not. The six and one-fourth hours' television watching (the American average per day) which non-reading children do is what is called alpha-level learning. The mind needn't make any pictures since the pictures are provided, so the mind cuts current as low as it can. It is somewhat parallel to the way the body, provided you sleep in enough blankets, will cut heat down as low as it can.

People who love to solve puzzles experience a kind of mental joy: so do people who hypothesize events which have not happened and never will. "But just say!" cries Natalie, "That a family of bears *did* seriously move in next door, Dad?"

What the little girl is doing there, and why her face is so luminous as she waits for Dad's wild answer (she trusts him to make it wild) is this: she is *leaving the donnée*. Why, if the streets of Duluth could be peopled half with bears of the mild Minnesota-black-bear sort and half with people, why ever would anyone want to stick to having just people?

It is the mental-image-enjoying function which leads us away from the autobiographical instance we sprang from. The moment we realize we are free of *how it really happened*, we are absolutely delighted—and mysteriously, on the heels of such delight, come bounding moral judgment and aesthetic taste.

If we know a Vern and a LaVonne who met and married, but we decide that instead of just staying on as a rather slack, practical-minded engineer, Vern is going to be a whistle-blower, how did we ever decide on such a thing? Just preferring sailing to fossil-fuel-burning boats doesn't make an ethical whistle-blower out of anybody! We decided on it this way, I believe—but it must be a guess, because I am not a psychologist. I think that the moment we are processing or typing along and we change how it was to how it *might be*, the natural ethical tastes of our species jump in and begin "loading" the situation. Suddenly, something very electric in our minds, but which goes about under the boring title of "values," has entered. It joins the first-draft writer and starts steering the story.

That sounds like a happy work process. It is. There is other good news. Even though Natalie's parents did not provide her with early encouragement in things imaginative, she is not locked out. Children recover not only from childhood trauma but from aesthetic or ethical vacuum. Grown people can catch up some imaginative growth by reversing the process: just as a child makes a story and the story leads him or her to some *values*, an adult can deliberately list *values*, deliberately attach a true anecdote to each of them (generally such anecdotes are the first time the adult experienced something which brought out the value—e.g., watched someone torture a dog). Such a deliberate, conscious reversal does wonderful work for people whose childhoods passed without the joy of storytelling.

Making up stories increases one's love of the universe generally: everyone knows that. There isn't anyone who tells stories fast who doesn't feel joyful doing it. Happily, making up values listings and then letting the items on them lead us *back to story* also increases one's love of the universe.

CHAPTER ONE: NOTES

1. André Dubus, "A Father's Story," anthologized in *The Houghton Mifflin Anthology of Short Fiction*; ed. Patricia Hampl; Houghton Mifflin, Boston, 1989.

2. Janet Burroway, *Writing Fiction*, Little, Brown, Boston, 1987. "A Story is a War" is the title of the first chapter.

3. Mark Helprin, "The Schreuderspitze," in *The Houghton Mifflin Anthology of Short Fiction*.

4. Dylan Thomas, "Do Not Go Gentle Into That Good Night."

5. Leo Hertzel, "Five Answers to a Frowning Question," *Growing Up American: Record*, ed. Leo J. Hertzel and John P. Schifsky; The College of St. Scholastica, Duluth, 1989.

6. Peter Elbow, "Closing My Eyes As I Speak: An Argument for Ignoring Audience," *College English*, 49 (1), January, 1987, pp. 50–69.

7. Lawrence Kohlberg, *The Philosophy of Moral Development*, Harper & Row, New York, 1981.

8. C.S. Lewis, *The Abolition of Man: Reflections on Education with Special Reference to the Teaching of English in the Upper Forms of Schools*, Macmillan, New York, 1944.

9. Ernest Becker, *Revolution in Psychiatry*, The Free Press, New York, 1964, p. 130.

How to Generate Not Words But Emotional Content

Middle- and upper-middle-class Americans preserve an ob-
durate, standoffish attitude towards psychology and
psychotherapy and the wisdom of social workers. I at first
supposed this attitude to be natural residue of the nineteenth-
century attitudes towards crazy people. Then I blamed "the
medical model"—still much touted on the East Coast: no one
wants to be sick, so if the wisdom of psychology is a treatment of sick people, we don't need it around the house.

Psychology, so far as educated liberal-arts people in
powerful positions are concerned, is for losers. They don't see
the ingenious use we could make of it. As people worry about
German reunification, the old cries rise, "What if the Germans
should . . . etc., etc.?" For all the hard thinking that psychol-
ogists and sociologists have been doing about psychology and
the Germans, I have seen no evidence that State Department
types even know of their work. If Miller and Staub are right in
connecting how adults treat children (adults being Germans,
Americans, everybody) with why those children grow up to
engage, fairly equably, in genocide, we should alter our
schools and our education of parents so that we would not
rear children at risk to charismatic leaders who propose
genocide.

Here is a list of marvelous, wise, life-changing books,
some of whose content could alter how we raise our children.
The first three books offer insights in *normal psychology*—
how normal people behave so that evil results. The last three

35

books are texts in therapeutic ways to change the awarenesses of *normal people who have been dangerously unconscious.*

Alice Miller, *For Your Own Good: Hidden Cruelty in Child-Rearing and the Roots of Violence*, English edition translated by Hildegarde and Hunter Hannum. Farrar, Straus & Giroux Inc., New York, 1983.

Ervin Staub, *The Roots of Evil: the Origins of Genocide and Other Group Violence*, Cambridge University Press, Cambridge, 1989.

Peter Sichrovsky, *Born Guilty: Children of Nazi Families*, English edition translated by Jean Steinberg. Basic Books, New York, 1988.

Irving Janis, *Groupthink*, Houghton Mifflin, Boston, 1983.

Lawrence Shulman, *The Skills of Helping: Individuals and Groups*, 2nd Edition, Peacock, Itasca, IL 60143, 1984.

Irvin D. Yalom, *The Theory and Practice of Group Psychotherapy*, Basic Books, New York, 1970.

As soon as one reads the ideas of Miller, Staub, Sichrovsky, one recognizes that here are insights to help us. Here is something we can work with! We can make known all these ideas about how parents influence children, stunt them, discourage them, make them long for charismatic pseudo-parents, make them unconsciously long for scapegoats—and all the refinements. How useful to know about "moral drift"— that psychological phenomenon which takes place among absolutely normal, even classy people!

The American class system works against us. We are willing to acknowledge, now, that role modeling causes evil. We know that the six and one-fourth hours' daily TV watching of average Americans is making them violent in part because they watch an estimated 144 murders during each day. They experience "moral drift." In the movies, violence seems usual to its perpetrators and to the police, so it becomes usual to viewers.

Most Andover and Yale graduates will grant this role-modeling a likely psycho-social phenomenon in the United States today. Let us imagine *one* Andover and Yale graduate, since we are practicing literature—the art of the *single example*, not of summaries.

Let us make our Andover grad be a man named Peter Tenebray. (I chose Tenebray for his last name because it is pronounced like *tenebrae*, shadows in Latin and the name of a Church of England service for Thursday and Friday before Easter which is very pensive. C.G. Jung would say Peter Tenebray was full of shadow: nearly everything difficult inside him he has shoved into unconsciousness.)

If I say to Peter, "We are all kept unconscious by the group whose values we accept without question. Educated people, for example, do not question or discuss one another's ethical commitments and unethical behaviors *in their corporations*. Wives do not ask their husbands why they let themselves agree to sell all the forests to Japan, or why they sell weapons to Iran, or why they keep contracting for expensive weaponry when the poor are desperate and the earth needs care."

Peter will look solemn and answer civilly. Then a light joke—not in a jeering tone, either. Peter is not Donny in the used-car lot. "I certainly am glad wives don't climb into bed with ethical questions!" he says with a smile. "In fact, one of the marvelous aspects of marriage is that no one said you had to talk about one another's ethics or lack of ethics!"

What interests me in this exchange is that Peter is using *his class background* to defend himself from moral change just as irrevocably as Donny used *his*. And both men's wives have apparently agreed not to question their husbands' parts in the world's troubles. (So far, at least. Later we will see that Peter's wife, Natalie, does question Peter.)

It is very hard for otherwise sophisticated, educated people to acknowledge that someone else's field has more to offer the public weal than their own. I think we need to know, in the 1990s, that developmental psychology and psychotherapy and the therapeutic part of social-work practice have at least as much to offer the *res publica* as American literature. How wasteful we are if we do not learn all we can of these people's savvy. It means giving up the reckless habit of simply reading in one's own field. Many of us remember the nutritionist Adelle Davis, whose books were charming and helpful. But I remember that Davis suggested that if you had a preteen girl being petulant and ill-tempered around the house, you could save yourself some trouble by dosing her up with extra calcium. What Davis was doing there was meeting a challenge with such skill as *her own profession* could offer when what was wanted was the Women's Movement. Eleven-year-old girls found out, in the 1950s, that their ebullience in sports, their imaginative play, their enthusiasm for nature was going to *lessen*, not strengthen, people's respect for them as they entered their teens. Now that was a very disappointing discovery. It is psychological injustice, which Adelle Davis ignored.

As we look at the reunification of Germany and the increasing violence elsewhere, we should ask if it is reckless of us to treat the Germans with the same old *political science* insights when they need to be treated with *psychological* insights.

All this to say that much of psychology can be usefully practiced in writing literature. In this chapter, we will use a consciousness-raising technique which I made up for the National Farmers' Union American Farm Project, in 1975. I have been using it with creative-writing students ever since. Its supposition is that human beings are programmed for *ethical consciousness*: we can keep that ethical consciousness serviceable to us despite our junk culture of the 1980s and 1990s. This technique is called making a Values Listing. It happens to be a great help to writers of first drafts of stories.

Values Listing: Why Write One?

If literary analysis is not the right gear for people starting off writing short stories, what is?

Deliberate, precise consciousness-raising helps. There are dozens of writing manuals describing consciousness-raising by association. For example, you write down some words, then cluster others around those words—the subsequent writing generated by informal association. I prefer listing one's values to listing just words, because values are by definition emotional: they are how we *feel* about the given subject. It helps our always-mangy memory, in any case, to list the qualities of people or of life which we hold dear or which we deplore. A values listing keeps us conscious of *large* virtues when we can so easily get lost in *small* virtues. There must be, for example, thousands of CIA executives who greet every elevator operator and garden-upkeep person in and about their buildings every morning and evening. I have known only four people who I knew to be CIA people: two of them greeted elevator operators by name, warmly. If 50% of people in a profession known for unscrupulous behavior are kindly practicing small virtues, might 50% of writers not be practicing the small virtues of our trade—lovely phrasing, good metaphor, snappy dialogue—and committing the large vices of our trade—churning out plots full of people who role-model avarice and violence and who have no sense of world community?

Here is the model of values listing I use. I expect it could be improved.

Values Listing: Examples

1. Two goals or values which make life good or bearable or would if they were in operation.

2. Two goals or values which cause injustice and suffering or lessening of joy.

3. Two missing goals or behaviors. As a child, you thought grown-up life would have these. Now that you are adult, you don't see them around. In my case, one of these missing values is *intelligent conversation among men*. I was

brought up in a household with several men in it who talked seriously and humorously a lot of the time. Nothing suggested to me that men in other families could be so boring their conversations would make tears squeeze out of your eyes. I knew grown women were boring because I had heard more of their conversations. Then I grew up and heard men and women talking together, sometimes dully, sometimes brightly—and until I was thirty-five still somehow had the feeling that men talked mysteriously, philosophically, together. It might have been from so much reading of Erich Maria Remarque.

When I was thirty-five, I was asked to talk to a small-town Kiwanis group. I was good enough to be their speaker but not good enough, being a woman, to eat with them. I ate my lunch at a counter behind a Sears Roebuck room divider. I told myself, Don't be angry: after all, Haydn sometimes had to play from behind a screen. Royalty wanted to hear but not see musicians. I listened to the men sing old hymns, which they did beautifully. Then I eavesdropped on their talk, which gave me the idea of the missing values.

4. Two injustices which you see about you and should keep an eye on, even on your wedding day.

Obviously, whichever eight values one lists one day, one might like to change next week. The good of having a Values Listing is that at any one time, you have it, written down, *explicitly*. You are *clear* on your standing on those issues. Here is an example of how this helps writers: let's say you have written down (at least, *I* have) under *Bad* "the fact that not individual people but large corporations, groups, and government agencies do the terrifying evil of our time. In fact, organizations—not we individual people—endanger the earth itself. Yet, top level members of these organizations and the spouses who sleep with them, apparently feel no remorse. They are short-term profiting off the earth." That happens to be the most heartfelt of my Values List.

Let us say I am a beginning writer. I have written down that value. Then I set myself to write a short story. I do the things people have done, generally, in the short story: I talk about other people's *personal home lives* or, if they have no homes, I talk about their *personal homeless lives*. I do not write up a corporate person, in his office, causing the evil—even though that evil is one of the eight most interesting ethical items in my mind!

It is the *habit* of American and British literature *not* to handle corporate, group, and government evil in stories. And when we write fiction about a powerful man's life, we seldom have his wife Natalie thinking, as she adjusts her peignoir, "Peter is so comfortable—sweet and comfortable and bearlike, I think it is horrible of me to get tense in bed. If he has to make chemical weapons, well, then he has to, doesn't he? I suppose he does! I can't harass him about it, can I? Aren't I his *wife*?" (Perhaps later, because she and Peter don't straighten this out, *she* takes to drink? *He* takes to drink? She runs away? No, there's the money . . . *she* takes to drink because she hates what Peter does, but her marriage to him is the best investment she could make . . . Yes—*she* takes to drink.)

If I have written down my value, I may, like Odysseus, stay clear of the siren song of conventional literature. A sissy compunction of my intellect snorts, "Yeah, well you haven't any *experience* with upper-level execs who run these so-called evil corporate ventures!" I need to stand up to that voice and say, "Right, but I haven't any firsthand experience of death, either; I freely write about it anyway, as did Tolstoy."

If the Values Listing wants amending by next week, simply write in the amendment. People who are able to write down eight serious values won't be likely to write lying or shallow literature without noticing what they're doing. Noticing may make an enormous difference.

Writing a 3,000-to-10,000-Word Autobiography

From 1980 to 1988, I taught short-story writing at various workshops at Hamline University and the University of Minnesota, asking writers in the class to write their own autobiographies at the beginning of the term. I required only a half page of autobiography as a help to me in getting a little idea of each writer's interests. In 1987, I announced to several courses that the writers were to do a 3,000-to-10,000-word autobiography over the first weekend and hand it in at the next class meeting. Anyone feeling stuck might call me at home at any time before 10 p.m. on any night of the weekend. Anyone who reached my tape would get a call back from me. Anyone who found his or her autobiography going over 3,000 words *must* call, so I would have a chance to schedule more time for reading the longer manuscripts. No autobiography was to go over 10,000 words. If writers found themselves needing over 10,000 words, they had to cut—but only down to 10,000 words. They could keep the 10,000. I suggested they keep (for themselves) the overflow passages as well. Retyping old journals doesn't do the equivalent psychological *work*. The prevailing intelligence of the author, his or her confidence that this life of one's own is a real life, comes only from writing autobiography deliberately after the fact. We all know, of course, that sexual intercourse can be lovely in places other than under the Eiffel Tower: we know that rationally, but thousands of people who write all their lives have the illusion that their town, their yard, their husband or wife, their workplace, are not so literary as Flaubert's.

The autobiography does less good if it is all about childhood. The psychological reasoning here is that everyone knows that *feeling attaches to childhood*. That's why we get so many "moving" memoirs about old Christmases. What writers need to know is that feeling attaches to adulthood, and not just to the famous moments either, such as when that odd curl of round lumpy baby, veined over with one's own birthblood, waits for you to hold it and welcome it to our universe. Chekhov was the genius of the slight moment: you look deeply into the eyes of someone you're in love with and suddenly you see—just for a moment, of course—no kindly disposed person would stick with such an idea—that the loved person is crazy or dumb. To catch minor experience, one needs a deliberate, intellectual autobiography-writing.

It needs to be at least 3,000 words so it makes up such a

large piece of writing that it exhausts the clichés one has been dishing up for previous teachers who gullibly allowed that "500 words would be OK." If one does a 500-worder in college twice, three times in graduate school, plus several times in slack but cheery summer writing camps, one has crystallized some clichés about oneself. The 3,000-word boot-camp requirement drives the consciousness to remember afresh: one can't simply spruce up the same old maunderings one has offered up over coffee, in intentional groups, or at family reunions. That lot gets said in 900 words: there are 2,100 still to go! The sleepy lion of the subconscious hears our *cri de coeur*: "What shall I say? Twenty-one hundred more words!" It hears that cry and is pleased to totter to its feet. "Here are events," the lion growls, *"and* feelings, both of which you have ignored until now."

Those who call on the weekend and ask if it is OK to go to 10,000 words nearly always are those who had assured me and their classmates that they had no material for an autobiography. They, especially, need to write a long autobiography. They have repressed their lives. If they don't do the autobiography fully now, their unconscious desire to *have* a life will keep interfering with their fiction. The unconscious will keep shrieking, "Look at *me*! Don't look at *other* characters! There's *me* you must look at!"

So we try to knock off the autobiography before trying short stories.

A word about student writers who want to write from their fancy—parable or science fiction. Both parable and science fiction are almost always morally based: that is, the author has an ethical or psychologically insightful idea to lay, in fictional form, before the reader so the reader will learn. That is what Jesus did with his parables; it is what all religious storytellers do with their parables. It is what most science-fiction writers do. Parables and science fiction make wholesome enough yarns, but they fail both writer and reader in a good many ways, too. Here is how: when Jesus or anyone else told a parable, the whole plot of it was thought up ahead, with a limited purpose in mind: teaching others *an idea the author had already explored*. It is therefore logical, but way oversimplified material. Preachy, too. Oversimplification, even stereotypicality, are the disservice of the parable to the reader, but in this book we are concerned with writers, not readers, so let's look at the disservice to the writer: by planning the outcome firmly, the writer has locked out any learning which his or her unconscious, intuitive mind might lend the story as the first draft goes along. Second, parable and science-fiction writers don't use their own material: they use collective culture—what we know of mustard seeds, capital investment (talent burying), hiring unreliable servants, etc., as their material. Parable material is by nature collective—generic. Science-fiction material is even less specific to life as we know it, because the factual settings are usually fabricated. Both forms, then, lock out the growth we writers make when we *reflect on our own specific experience*.

Thousands of idealists want to write modern folktales (parables, really) and science-fiction parables although the authors aren't technology buffs. They enter short-story-writing classes with that in mind. They are understandably cross, therefore, when told that every serious, literary endeavor springs at least partly from some realism—our willingness to use here some pieces, there some pieces, of our own lives. And worse, they have to write an autobiography.

I noticed that those who have written what felt like a fullish autobiography are later able to do the following:

1. They respect their own lives. They trust *their own material* as acceptable material for short fiction.

2. They leave their *données* comparatively easily. That is, they have had a chance to dwell upon their own life, so it doesn't keep calling out to them, "Look at this! Look at this! And *this!*" in the way it did before they got out the autobiography. Indeed, instead of clinging to the actualities of their own experience, they now rejoice in a chance to spring away from it toward whatever *second element* might snag in their weir.

3. They write with more love of our universe and our lives in general, however beleaguered their own circum-

stances. Anything we recognize the *details* of, we tend to *like* a little better. People who have written their autobiographies *like* their own lives better than they did before they set them down in words. (This is not *always* a blessing: old militarists often do memoirs in which they seem to fall in love with the wretched killings they organized and carried out. Because killing made up 60% of the purpose of their lives, and their lives have become dear to them, they tend to recall killing with a kind of tenderness—of course, with the caveat—the attractive, grave caveat— "we don't like everything soldiers must do" posture. Very few people write an autobiography in which they disparage the lifelong evil they have conducted.)

To be certain of my conclusions about writing autobiographies, I recently conducted a "control group": that is, I taught one class at the University of Minnesota on how to write short stories without requiring the autobiography and another class in which I did require it.

Those who did the long autobiography were finally ready to leave off being delighted with self-expression for its own sake. They could turn their eyes outward and notice other human beings with amusement, gratitude, fury, or love. They became willing to question their characters. "What kind of a person are you?" we ask the mean mom. "What else have you done besides impact on that poor child (the writer)?" You find that the cruel mother runs a class at the Community Ed Center for sailboat-model building, helping those landlocked Lutherans make beautiful stays and shrouds of stiffened thread! Now the mother has at least two selves: mean mom and good community person (like Dickens's Mrs. Pardiggle). Let's look at the scene again:

"You're Vern's mom? You teach all those people to make sailboats?"

Vern's mom then gives some technical description. Repressed people love technical details; if you say to a repressed person, "What do old ships *mean* in your life?" they just stare, but if you say, "What is that poor sailor on the poop deck doing?'' they brighten and say, ''O—he's holystoning the deck!''

An obvious good in literature is to see several sides of a character—bad mum, good teacher. Another good of getting past what we know of someone from mere life is that sooner or later we shall have to cut a good many characters out of a short-story manuscript. If we have our cousins and uncles and grandchildren and the German Shepherds of our childhood and rotten third-grade teachers in our Autobiography, well and good: to get the intensity of them into a short story, we shall have to combine several of them. The sooner one gets used to this idea, the sooner one can write a story.

It helps some people to fake a little confrontation with a relative or two. ''Sorry, Vern's Mom, but you don't get into my story. There isn't room. I am taking your love of sailboats, however, and putting it into your son Vern, because he is going to be a person with good tastes in boating.''

Tolstoy knew dozens of people who resembled Ivan Ilyich (in *The Death of Ivan Ilyich*). He knew dozens of peasants like Gerasim, who did the humble physical care of Ivan Ilyich in the last weeks of his life. Gerasim was not subtle and devious and in no sense splendid. Tolstoy's achievement in the relationship of Ivan Ilyich and Gerasim is in seeing that the master preferred this good man in his last weeks: he didn't want his aristocratic or nearly-aristocratic family and friends bothering him.

To arrive at that insight, Tolstoy did two psychological exercises appropriate to First-Draft-Stage writing: he left the *donnée*. Since Tolstoy himself had not gotten sickened to death, we know he left his own life. He looked outward at Gerasim, and then pretended that he himself was Ivan Ilyich, a bored man, a jerk, a man rude to his wife, a longtime sellout to the bureaucracy, an unoriginal, slavish adherent of middle-brow cultural tastes. Then Tolstoy did the *second* psychological exercise which interests me: he asked himself, if I were like Ivan Ilyich, what exactly might still waken my spirit? Something numinous, something not cynical. Ah—I might, at last, at the eleventh hour, learn to love a good man. It gives the story its *only* light. The literary good of it is that light shows up all the ghastly human waste presented in the rest of the story.

Until we are free of our own autobiography, our self-absorption, we are like a girl who keeps going around with the high-school sweetheart who is mildly living along, doing a little hunting in the fall, wrapping toxic-chemical cans in newspaper with scotchtape so the garbage collector will pick it up without knowing, getting jobs whacking bush under the high-power lines. Then she meets a grown, thinking man but doesn't recognize the meaning in him.

There are two kinds of social pressure in the 1990s about autobiography: women are socialized to write it, in order to hear our own voices over men's voices of mild insult, so that all insult is *outside*, instead of *inside*, us. Women have to confront males about their rudeness and injustice. Women must write our history (as blacks do theirs), so we have it—the way an athlete must have muscle. Men, on the other hand, are socialized *not* to write autobiography because it is not an extroverted activity. People pretend that males are allowed to be introverts, but in fact they are not: they must, to be successful in our truly externalized society, join and manage and control organizations of one kind or another, which requires of them 1) technocratic behavior and 2) extroversion. Treachery in business, or in squeezing some other professional out of grants, secrecy, and crisp, sensible lying are *de rigueur*. None of those qualities is attractive, so we use other language about them, e.g., males must be assertive and empowered, and so on. If males wrote autobiography, they would see psychological truths such as the psychological fact that male initiation, driving boys into groups with men away from love (the home) and into some half- if not wholly-hostile organizations (hunters' groups, fraternities, the Navy, good prep schools, men's 'groups'), is not good, but bad. It accommodates the predator and suppresses affection. So males write very little autobiography, and I have never met a male outside of Philosophy and English classes and National Endowment for the Humanities projects who has written a Values Listing.

I make mention of these pressures in the hopes that people will recognize them and shake their souls free of them. It is gross, I think, that young men should be prevailed upon to become hasty, valueless people—easily suborned into wicked work in large groups. Unmitigated extroversion means such lack of personal values. The *Volkspolizei* of East Germany were deliberately recruited from Saxon farm boys—that is, young people who didn't talk values at home so they had a kind of ethical vacuum. Their police-school masters could fill that ethical vacuum with such bullying ideas as they liked. "The ideal CIA recruit is 'externalized': more oriented towards doing than planning and towards trial-and-error methods than careful conceptualization. He or she is 'adaptable' in social situations: charming, outgoing, able to meet other people's expectations, a bit of a chameleon."[1] George Orwell was partly right in showing us how the black pig made off with the young puppies and trained them into stormtroopers: a missing truth is that all you really need for evil to happen is a sizable population of people not thinking up their own Values Listing. Unconsciousness is as serious as evil training—and its catchment-area appears to be by far and away mostly men of eighteen to thirty. They wake, rubbing their eyes, in the Marine Corps or the CIA.

If you find yourself balking at practicing the artifices which make the short story, if you find yourself crying, "But that sounds like literary tricks! That is manipulative!" it may mean you should do a short memoir or essay right now. No one's soul is quite free when some new sharp insight into one's own life has just been served up. Here is an embarrassing example. For a little over two years, I have been trying to put together my life with a martinet of an aunt during World War II, with my childhood fear of the Gestapo and my childhood habit of drawing soldiers bayonetting other soldiers, with my art lessons given me by the painter Stella Sassoon. I have wrested this and that detail from memory, old furious memories, and forced everything together. At last my editor Ted Solotaroff suggested that this material wasn't coming along as *story*.[2] It was still just intelligent thinking.

The moral of this is that one can serve two masters, but not three: one can have personal values and intend to express them in literature. One can have a life history and intend to use large blocks of it, as is, in literature. Finally, one can want to make a story which is complete in itself. One can do any two of these things.

Like my students, I needed to be sent back to do more autobiography. The world is full of people who are, psychologically speaking, slowpokes. One has to forgive oneself!

A last word on autobiography writing: writers who do it faithfully, at least 3,000 words, will leave off all the sooner the idea that artistic device spoils one's heart's truth. It doesn't. It makes a manuscript *carry* that heart's truth in a small, symbolic, dense package. Autobiography writers sooner leave off using phrases like "find out who I am" and they leave off pretending that "male, linear thinking" is really male or really lamentable. They absolutely stop referring to their own writing as "my garbage" or "my shit."

They are poised to do the work that artists do.

The First Draft as Generation

When you mean to steal an idea from someone else, not just the idea but even the phrasing of it, it is best to do it straight off. I am stealing the following idea from poet, memoirist and teacher Patricia Hampl:[3]

> *Idea*: First you do generation *without organizing*.
> Later you get to the organization. Not till later!

The genius of Hampl's idea is that you must lengthen the time given to generation-without-efforts-to-shape. The skills of organization are not wanted in the first draft.

Some writing classes start, using peer critiquing—a mixed bag at best—helping one another *organize* even before the author has discovered the true heart of the story. In the first draft, the author should still be brooding, maundering around the material—treating it like a *hypothetical* first draft. It is a great mistake at that point to start "applying writing skills" or anything like.

Sometimes students who have read how-to-write manuals or have taken writing courses in noncollegiate writing classes tell me, "Here is my first draft: I know it needs polishing, of course. Help me polish my skills." The writer should have said, "Here is my first draft." Then my job, as teacher, is to role-play the job the writer must do—ask questions. What else did this character do? Who's *he*? Where was all this? Did you say when this was? What else about these people? Are you sure *that's* all he felt? Did he feel a second feeling too?

The skills of generation are questioning . . . inviting the unconscious to join. Be certain *not to cut anything.* If things don't fit, save them for the future.

Yet here is a warning. It comes from the field of psychotherapy: follow the strong feeling—never mind if it is inconsistent. In other words, delight and fury may run together in your first draft: never mind wondering or doubting it. But don't let yourself do mindless low-key association where you don't feel anything. Don't gas on and call it associative writing.

I suggest not beginning with any of the prewriting schema which sometimes work for essays—clustering, circles—other free-association formats. There is a laxity about them which might let you slide through twenty or thirty pages: you might forget the one discipline you need in the first draft: to follow where anger, or delight, or laughing take you. What if Mansfield, in her first draft of "Bliss" had allowed herself to go on for two or three pages about the omelette which Bertha ordered up and Harry praised? Well, what harm in that? we might ask—she can cut it out later during the Organization stage of the writing. Not so. If you go off on a no-feeling tendril, such as how Bertha's omelette served to the uneasy husband reminds her of omelettes her mother made for her, your unconscious, which you are trying to bait, really—draw into the snare of work—will say to itself, "O—right! More low-key anecdotes. Back to sleep, fellows." (Fellows, not fellow, since the unconscious, like the devil, is legion.)

To sum up: in the *generation* stage of your writing follow intensity wherever it takes you. If you feel no intensity, pull out your Values Listing. Looking down it, ask yourself, What scene or event in my life made me write down *that* particular value? Who had done *what* that I was so struck as to draw a principle from it? Recall the time and places. We need to be reminded that when we *draw a universal value* out of something, it means we *felt* something—and that's the material we want for our story. If we can recall the specifics of the afternoon and the deck or shore or bed where we felt it first, then we can write again. (It is very wise never to use the words *writers' block:* it gives professional dignity to what is really either sloth, or so much enjoyment of life itself at the moment, why write literature? or an Eichmann-like unconsciousness of human grief.)

First Draft: Practicing Containment

Practicing containment is a Jungian idea meaning mulling over one's deliberations without talking about them to other people. When Mary "pondered all these things in her heart," she was practicing containment. We don't want other voices while writing the first draft of any story. Besides, all offers of help with the first draft are not so friendly as they sound. There are many friends to unfinished craft, few to unfinished art. I have made several quilts, three small buildings, one brick walk, dozens of doll clothes, dozens of hand-knitting-machine clothes for children: I have never shown the roughed-out pieces for quilts, the studs and endposts or the cut rafters for a shack, the 590 pattern for bricks, or the knit socks still without their toes and heels and received jeering or damnation through faint praise. When I have shown people (when I used to make this mistake) first drafts of literature, on the other hand, I realized art is taken, however unconsciously, as an enemy by a good many people who are genuine friends. This may be explained as Yi-Fu Tuan does, in his *Segmented Worlds and Self:* people intuitively suspect that thinkers-about-ordinary-life sooner or later will become changers: they start up all that thinking and next thing you know, they have unearthed some supposed injustice in what was just a really nice community without trouble, and now look—trouble.[4] (I have made a reckless précis of one of Yi-Fu Tuan's observations here.) Dislike of reflectiveness is usually unconscious, which means you will suddenly hear some hostile remarks in very surprising places. I think that teachers of writing should refuse to see first drafts of creative work.

Most Americans think of writing classes as support groups—which means, not much artistic discipline is offered around as someone reads aloud from a work in progress. Support groups are marvelous when one is writing the 10,000-word autobiography, because there isn't a human being for whom a thoroughgoing memory of the past doesn't bring up some intense feeling. For that, friendship is lovely. At the point where you want to make a universal work of art, however, organized around some notion bigger than your own life, I'd drop out of the writers' group or read them something else. You can read creative nonfiction. It is pleasant, and it doesn't put your group on the spot. Support groups can't help you do *art* at the first-draft level.

A second reason for staying private during the generation of your story material: many friends who like "feelings" in truth like only mild feelings. They are rattled the moment they find you writing something *intense:* namely, you are trying to make literature. It is very separating.

Serious artistic work divides family at just this moment. There are three groups of people who have a considerable stake—psychologically, that is—in your *not* succeeding at writing literature: they are your relations, neighbors, and your clergy. They know, in their inchoate way, that if you make a serious work of art, you are independent of them. You will have stepped into your own dinghy. They've lost you as minion or codependent. Besides, even in America, where people assume the prestige goes to money, corporate power, and those who get tax money for weaponry, the psychological truth is people are also envious of artists, especially of writers. Quite appropriately, everyone wants to be a writer. It is naïve to say, "Oh, but my family *want* me to succeed!" They may or they may not resent you. If you are doing the first draft, I wouldn't trust your family so far as you can throw a piece of string.

Third, the most inward and therefore the best reason: your soul needs to be lonely so that its strangest elements can moil about, curl and growl and jump, fail and get triumphant, all inside you. Sociable people have the most trouble hearing their unconscious. They have trouble getting rid of clichés because clichés are sociable. They can't penetrate their own hypocrisies. They tend to hear their souls as one voice, not the several voices they sometimes are. If you yourself spent a childhood in team games and Little League activities, with little unplanned solitude, you will have a hard time sinking into the *second element* of a story. It can be done. To reassure your unconscious that you are serious, abandon your buddies.

CHAPTER TWO: NOTES

1. Melissa Everett, *Breaking Ranks*, New Society Publishers, 4527 Springfield Avenue, Philadelphia, PA 19143, 1989, page 63.

2. Ted Solotaroff, Senior Consulting Editor, Harper & Row, author of *The Red Hot* and *A Few Good Voices*.

3. Patricia Hampl, author of *A Romantic Education*, *Spillville*, editor of *The Houghton Mifflin Anthology of Short Fiction* (1989), professor in the Creative Writing Department, University of Minnesota Department of English (Minneapolis).

4. Yi-Fu Tuan, *Segmented Worlds and Self*, University of Minnesota Press, Minneapolis, 1982.

Plot and Subplot

Getting to Plot

The Loft, a Minneapolis-based writers' organization, asks out-of-town authors to be apprenticeship masters for Loft members. Two psychological clouds thicken around these nationally recognized "mentors" and the writers who want to learn from them: first, The Loft itself is an organization which recognizes *generation of material* as absolutely the most important part of making literature. Cut-and-slash critiquing—urging writers to learn something called "craft" more quickly—is anathema to generation. The Loft has a fifteen-year tradition of gentleness with other people's hearts' truths. This gentleness irritates technocrats. It enrages writing teachers who take pride in up-down relationships with their students. (It is as with doctors: there are still doctors who let their receptionists and even nurses say, "Doctor says . . . " or "Doctor isn't in . . . ," or, "You will have to ask Doctor.") Those are people to whom power means more than brother-hood or sisterhood among us all. I resist feeling alarmed about them: they have a long tradition, from well before Pharaoh, of expecting to enjoy feeling superior to others. They *do* enjoy feeling superior to others, too. It isn't a sensual pleasure, but it is a pleasure of long standing.

The second psychological irritation of the mentors is with writers who can't present a story character *doing* anything. One mentor told me, "Minnesota writers are forever setting a character on a lakeshore and then leaving him or her there to think some interior monologue while squinting out over the water. That's not literature: that's just journal robbings." She was right: journal robbings, to be literature, must be transformed into plot or they need the crusty presence of a real *idea*. We take that problem up in this chapter.

Since there are 17,000—7,000 more than the alleged 10,000—lakes in Minnesota, it stands to reason that Minnesota writers join the other four million Minnesotans in squinting out over one or more of these lakes from time to time. Doing some reflection on life while squinting out over a lake is endemic to Minnesotans, the way watching the waves make and then destroy the lace and purfling of foam is to people from Inverness, Castine, and Cape Ann.

We are people who, like Socrates, know that the examined life is indeed the one worth living, but now we want to write a short story, that starts with squinting out over a lake. Nebraskans and Arizonans must forgive my using the lake-squinting as a sample.

Here is a start. I have put in a person who is not I. I am consciously trying to leave my self out for now. I want to see others.

> When LaVonne had jammed the hook through the worm's length, she squinted out over the lake and said to herself, "Just like Vern to forget to grease the Evinrude on our anniversary."

There is a measure of ugliness in that sentence—not uncommon in first drafts of anything. When I get ugly, I try to check over the Values Listing. Somewhere in it, I recorded being afraid that corporations or governments will destroy the environment for their own profit. For example, what if American corporations sell, in addition to huge tracts of North American forest they have *already* sold to the Japanese (who are warehousing all that lumber against the profitable day when there is much less lumber about), all of the rest of the trees as well? How can I, who don't retain a lawyer, protect the trees against such corporations or governments? Those corporations and governments are married to each other with their lawyers as bridesmaids and ushers. I wake in the night with the Planet

Horrors—a malaise Tolstoy never had to fret over. All he, lucky author, had to worry about was

the rich being cruel to the poor;

the mindless wars to which nice regimental types might be sent and subsequently mindlessly maimed or killed;

that one might not find one's true love in life.

In the first paragraph of *Resurrection*, Tolstoy says that although the grown people continued manipulating one another for profit and throwing pollution (naphtha in his day) into the air and not noticing the beautiful day which God gave everyone to rejoice in, the birds sang, etc. We can't relax like Tolstoy. Rachel Carson didn't live in vain: we know spring itself might be wrecked by corporations.

I bring this up with purpose. If we do not admit utterly consciously that we are both angry and anxious a good deal of the time, specifically at organizations endangering the world, we will not write a literature good for anything except escape.

Escape has its value, of course, like dessert: it is not food, but it is fun, and harmless if you have eaten real food first. It slightly corrupts one's tastes. People who do too much escape reading and all writers who do a lot of escape writing eventually lose their moral sense. Perhaps they meant to. Life is calmer without any moral sense. I allow myself escape literature every night before falling asleep: I read Maugham because his stories take place among toffs and fakes and English drivel and corny values, and best of all, they take place *back then* not to mention *far away*—what better escape! Maugham did not write afraid of the H-bomb. He worried little about the twentieth century's dangerous personality type—the man willing, as the NASA and Morton Thiokol people put it, to "remove his engineer's hat and put on his management (profit-considering) hat"; Maugham's few characters of that sort had such small purlieu: their evils fell upon the helpless of *their* time and very few of them. So Maugham's stories work is escape for me.

A second reason I bring up consciousness of gross

injustice is that if we try to write stories as if we were not thinking of those people who sell the woods and poison the air, our wrath and fear leak upward from our unconscious in spurts where we don't want it—and what's more, sometimes show up as a readiness to be snide.

Let's look again at the first sentence about LaVonne by the lakeside: What kind of a person did I choose to do this story about? Someone who "jammed a hook through the whole length" of another creature's body. Someone like Jude's wife in *Jude the Obscure*. And what slumping idea of marriage has this person got? "Just like Vern to, etc., etc." Psychologically, Square One: people who array any one disappointment in the person they married against a smudged, general disillusionment with that *person*. "Just what he *always* does. On our anniversary, he doesn't grease the outboard." The author feels both superior and cross.

The cure is to say to myself, I am enraged about something. What is it? Well—I wrote a Values Listing. Drag it out and keep it before me throughout this story. What's on my Values Listing? A hatred of people who poison air and earth, among others. What did I list as a prevailing injustice: the fact that large powerful *groups* do the evil in our time, not individual people.

If I put someone in the story who has the same feelings, that character gives honor to those feelings. I feel relieved, having got that said, and I can go back to loving life itself. I want that, because love of life is what makes me *see* particulars, and then *write* particulars.

This is a first draft of a story which has so far only one sentence. Let's try the *last* sentence—to break the cliché. We have all been told *ad nauseam* that a story has a beginning, a middle, and an end—an absurd idea. To break that cliché, let's now write a tentative *ending* sentence, so that we have a second pier to stretch this rubber band on. Here it is—taken straight from my values listing:

> Vern might be out of a job, but he was not damn sorry. He watched a mother loon guide her young, following some accurate navigation of her own.

Two things have happened here: we have a nice man in the story. We have a nice creature of nature.

We will adjust some adjectives now, in order:

1. to give the story gracious tone—to bring in the idea of virtue, and

2. to tie in a specific idea from the Values Listing: the idea of safety in our universe.

So here is the first sentence and here is the last, with it:

> When LaVonne had jammed the hook through the worm's length, she squinted out over St. Fursey lake and said to herself, "Just like Vern to forget to grease the Evinrude on our anniversary."
> . . . . . . (Story) . . . . . .
> Vern might be out of a job, but he was not damn sorry. He watched a mother loon guide her young, following some accurate navigation of her own.

We know that somewhere in that story, Vern did something he is proud of, and in some way it is germane to the loon, who like Vern gets anxious about safety.

It is important to drop most of what you have heard about morality spoiling fiction. All the good fiction has moral charge like electric charge. What bores people is not morality but lack of morality. Churches, for example, will never admit that their principal problem is moral boredom. They keep trying to hype the liturgies when the cause of the boredom is either aesthetic or ethical. Aesthetically, Catholics, for example, resent their slangy services; Episcopalians grieve for their elegant offbeat language, "very God of very God," so interesting, now washed down into "true God of true God," which is ordinary. Ethically, churches take so few stands against corporate evil, it's hard to justify paying them tithes. Those thousands of dollars are needed for lobby groups against corporate evil.

This twofold problem of aesthetic boredom and moral boredom is also the problem of literature. How shall we avoid the boredom of having LaVonne or Vern sitting by the lake? I added in a saint's name, a rather nice saint, too—Fursey, an abbot who saw visions "of the fires of falsehood, covetousness, discord, and injustice lying in wait to consume the world"—according to the Venerable Bede—visions which inspired late medieval thought—some light of which shows up in Dante's *Divine Comedy*.[1] It is not important to any reader that St. Fursey's name is attached to LaVonne's and Vern's lake: I, the writer, do it for myself to help offset the sneer I started off with.

Writing the last line of the story (which, of course, can be changed or discarded later) helps us gear up not for journal, nor poetry, but *plot*. Nothing else will do. Even Chekhov, who can build beautiful stories in which little happens except a couple of people walking, musing, or talking, meet some other people, or don't, would have some scene happen between the two sentences above.

Geometry is the science of the short-story writer—just as physics of the free and desperate sort is the science of poets. (I call twentieth-century physics free and desperate because it has shown us we have limited time left to live. We have four billion years, Stephen Hawkings tells us, which is a lot—but it is absolutely all. No more prayers ending "World without end, Amen." We are flying away from ourselves—we will inevitably cool and turn to cinder. If there is a God, that God did not plan an eternal party for us. It is the stuff of poetry.)

Trying a hypothesis to see if it will fit is the stuff of short-story plot. Let us try this hypothesis: Vern had a job at a nerve-gas lab. We know from the last sentence that he left the job and has a higher opinion of himself for having done so. We know it is his wedding anniversary and apparently he has a summer place on St. Fursey Lake. Some dullness has disappeared when we know that one of two lovers in the story has or had a job at a nerve-gas laboratory. The story has two possibilities for plot: 1) LaVonne's disrespect for Vern and 2) Vern's occupational idealism. One of these can be plot. The other can be subplot, perhaps.

The main plot of any story is like the strings of a violin, carefully made to bear the weight of bow and to transmit sound accurately. But a violin gets its *timbre* from the music box under the strings. Timbre, the resounding box in literature, is cultural allusion.

In the case of Vern, the sound box is his fear of evil. For all of us in the United States, the sound box of any literature we write is our fear and our undeniable national shame about our foreign policies[2]—but also, the past of places and the present facts about places we know. There is nothing new in all this. Cruel governments have always entered everyone's conscious or unconscious purview. Cruelties have always been the acid drop in lovers' joy. In the Values Listing, we listed a prevailing injustice or two going on in the background, even if this is our wedding day, going on without pause although it is Vern's and LaVonne's anniversary. Lovers squinting out over the great Nile knew that the morrow meant another twenty hours' unwanted hod-carrying for Pharaoh's gross projects. They must have partly felt the cruelty of slavery, even if slavery had eons of custom behind it. (At least they felt occupational stress.) If the lovers in *our* story are experiencing occupational stress, we are repressing relevant truth if we don't bring in the stress. Too simple a love life is an evasion— a denial—of our natural political life. That's one of the secrets of romance novels, of course: they contain love and no politics.

English Departments cling to psychological denial in order to avoid painful ideas. Writers catch denial like colds. Here is a passage by Michael True, in a review of David Perkins's *A History of Modern Poetry*:

> The meaning of *Howl*—Allen Ginsberg's and perhaps the period's principal poem—appears to have escaped him . . . Events such as the Cold War, the atomic bomb, the Vietnam War, imperial America and its presidencies, seem not to have existed in the literary historian's life-time—he writes about the period rather as if one wrote about Yeats without mentioning the Irish rebellion or about the early Eliot and Pound without mentioning the First World War . . . . . He (Perkins) prefers poetry that is meditative and general (one might say philosophic and vague), to poetry that names the griefs or joys, fears or hopes of a generation.[3]

True is dismayed that a major critic would choose not to think about how literature is our voice of ethical things. "Howl" is as much an ethicist's poem as an aesthete's.

Five Uses of Subplot

1. Subplot lets us bring in our ethical worries. Much is made of being in touch with one's sexuality: what if a good writer were constrained to be in touch with his or her ethicality?

2. Subplot helps us overcome the egocentricity of journal writing, memoir, and autobiography. We must have *second-level awarenesses*. One person's wedding day is the same day someone else has found out the disease they have isn't operable.

3. Subplot contrasts quality of feeling. LaVonne's feelings about Vern are shallow. A subplot lets us bring in someone more kindly than she—let's say someone named LeRoy, who filled LaVonne's tank at the Unocal 76 earlier that day. LeRoy has more elegance than LaVonne, let us say. In Shakespeare, Falstaff has more heart than Hal.

4. Subplot blessedly increases the actual number of events in a story. We won't give four whole paragraphs to someone's squinting out over a lake if we know that back at the nerve-gas lab, Vern has been fired for saying he didn't like what the chemists were manufacturing. Vern's boss, let's say, is a tough, middle-level executive named Duane Salaco. Duane works under the Andover/Yale man named Peter Tenebray. Duane said, "Vern, honey baby, listen to me. You know what I want you should do? I want you should go ahead and think anything you want to think. They ought to have an 800 conference exchange for people like you. You could all slop each other like

hogs in Iowa. Just get out of my office now, so I can make the call; I'll have your job filled in 20 minutes.''

Vern was so shattered he forgot his anniversary. He had promised to take his wife out fishing, and before they could do that, she said there was something about the boat motor. And no! she had snapped. You can't fish from your dumb sailboat! He forgot all of that. He went out past the rooms with tortured animals in them, imagining their rosy noses pressed against the wiring. Towards the end, the rabbits stopped screaming and twisting their bodies. They rolled over. The tiny jaws shuddered and pulled open. He once had the feeling the jaws moved a little after they died because they couldn't get said to us during their life what they felt, so they were still trying in the seconds after death.

5. Subplot can correct mistaken intentions of the author. Sometimes the subplot of drafts two, three, four, or even five, show us that what we have kept nailing up as the main plot was a mistake: the *true* story, the story close to us, is the subplot! We only just this moment noticed that! The conscious will had too recklessly arranged the main plot, with all the choices of character, tone, language, point of view, chronology. The less willful parts of our mind kept patiently laying the subplot before us. We need that less willful unconscious to make art.

I refer here only to that unconscious material close to the surface which luckily advises and blesses us from time to time. Let us say the author has set up a main plot and now says, "I will put some subcharacters in, who are doing something a little different." The instant an author says that, the near-unconscious lurches up from its constant if restless napping and cries, "Good! Here I am! I am rising to the occasion! I will do my great service to artists now! I will split the author's soul into its various voices and figures, and I will start a talk and dance among them all!"

There is surprising benefit in having our souls divided into their component voices. (It is, by the way, close to the benefit which people in psychotherapy experience when they learn to do "active imagination"—or set up a conversation between two or more parts of themselves: it lets you decide which voice is saying the best things for right now. We thus learn that not *all* voices in us have our general best interests at heart.)

Sometimes we authors are mistaken in whom we choose for the main character of any given story. In this story, we thought it was LaVonne. We gave her the first line, at least, and left her squinting out over St. Fursey Lake. But what if, somehow, she isn't the protagonist for us? Who else is around? There is LeRoy, for one, who was at the Unocal 76 station through long, sour hours earlier in the day. Now he is crowded into a VFW booth with some superficial acquaintance, a flaky humanities consultant—someone who keeps talking about "who we really are" but who can't be pinned down, the Genuine Parts fellow from St. Fursey (the town), and a girl he used to like whose name he ought to know but he keeps hoping someone will speak to her by name during the conversation so he will know, but they never say her name.

LeRoy is facing the fact that someone has stolen his wonderful black Labrador bitch Silver (I added in this dog because joy in pets was a *Good* on my Values Listing); LeRoy may never poke around Fursey Slough with Silver anymore because some goddamned bastard has stolen her. Right now, Silver must be missing him, too. She is not just businesslike like your average black lab: she loves LeRoy. Even in summer, when they didn't hunt, she kept beside him or in her sideways locktrot just in front of him, thoughtfully getting up the swamp birds—whatever was around—at the right range for his sixteen-gauge.

No one at the VFW pays much attention to LeRoy. He has never been much of a talker. One of the drinkers is shouting a lot, anyway. "Nerve gas!" he is shouting. "You betcha nerve gas! We need any kind of deterrent we got with those kind of people! So all them eastern European countries are falling off the Soviet Union, I'll believe it when I see it, if you ask me."

Someone else, who seems to emerge for a moment from a daydream of a different cast, now says: "Nature freaks! Listen, if they love nature so much, why don't they go live split-level in Fursey Slough?"

Suddenly the quiet LeRoy hears the words *Fursey Slough* and remembers he will never again poke around in Fursey Slough with Silver. They will never stop short to watch the otters play on their otter-slide. LeRoy rouses himself, squints across the smooth surface of the VFW booth table: he can make out through his drunkenness a bullying face, my God, that is an ugly face, of which the ugly mouth is just closing after having said something insulting about LeRoy's and Silver's slough. It occurs to LeRoy to give that ugly face a black eye so he reaches across the table and does it. For a moment, everything is much better.

That is not a wonderful incident, but it illustrates the third advantage of subplot. The author needed to get shed of LaVonne with her derisive temperament. Subplot writing brought forward LeRoy, who is a more sympathetic character than LaVonne. Subplot writing brought out Vern, LaVonne's husband, as a kind of ethical crux for the story. He may not be smart, but he's noble.

There are hazards in subplotting. The greatest of them is to have stock characters whom it is easy to make fun of. Mocking characters wrecks short-story writers: for every Maugham who feels like mocking but is so particular in his mockery that he half gets away with it, there are a thousand whose mockeries are clichés. We all know from our everyday life stock characters: that is because all classes of people except intellectuals tend to speak to one another largely in truisms: we don't exercise the complex social skills of telling each other things we are feeling on a deep level. We settle for hundreds of shallow conversations. The result is that whoever speaks most *colorfully* seems to be speaking most usefully from the point of view of a listener-author. Southern writers, whose dialogue has dense, gorgeous personality from the old rural south, often let themselves spend out the skein of their story in that gothic Southern "color." Flannery O'Connor allowed herself that luxury: it made her stories colorful and lively, but too often it substituted surface color for numinous quality. I do not join the thousands who regard "A Good Man is Hard to Find" as a marvelous story: I think the author is doing a regular Ellery Queen Magazine horror story, with her good ear for Southern Gothic dialogue making it sound more full of message than it is. It is a temptation, if one has known vivid conversationalists with despicable behavior habits. Much of Shakespeare's dialogue among the lowlifes is wonderful, and much of it is just stock-character writing.

I was raised in North Carolina: I know the temptation to stuff the sock of story full of this kind of thing: "Emma Jean, I want you should take them rabbits over to Miz Ravenal and you tell her I want forty-two cents a foot each except that one which the front feet got caught in Wayland's Coast to Coast router, which she can give me thirty-eight cents for, but this time she has to pay in regular U.S.A. tender and not send you home with an I.O.U. on Air Mail stationery."

When I was a graduate student at Minnesota, I took a fiction course from Allen Tate. I turned in a story about some lowlifes in Beaufort, South Carolina, and Allen read it aloud. He loved it. A man in a back row complained that the story really just made use of a Southern Gothic kit which anyone could come up with. Allen was furious. He put the man down fast, but not so fast that I didn't realize the man was right. I was twenty-five and cowardly. I did not stand up to our famous teacher and poet and defend the truth of the man in back. I owe this to that man: ever since, I have tried to remember to get rid of the faked-up stock dialogue which is easy to hasten our first-drafts with.

The current temptations in stock subplot characters seem to be

Prayer-Meeting and US Air Force personnel with Southern accents which come with the job

First-person narrators using Midwestern teen-talk (Holden Caulfield saying "pretty sure" and "I guess" in there instead of "goddam this" and "goddam that")

Fake Native American metaphoric talk

The way to discern whether we are filling in a subplot full of lowlifes instead of people who are really parts of ourselves is to ask, "Is there some part of me that wants forty-two cents a foot for some dead rabbits and thirty-eight cents for a shattered one?"

There is not. Therefore, to put Emma Jean, her mother, and Mrs. Ravenal into my story is not true subplot. It is settling into the swamp of local color.

If I seriously want Emma Jean in the story, I can check back to my Values Listing and find out if either of those two characters, with their print aprons full of dead animals, can enact any of the values I have. If they can, then we can reconsider that incident, or at least the two people in it, as material for story.

The best way to plan subplot is to recall the metaphor of the main plot being the violin's strings; and the cultural background, the issues, the physical past, and indeed future fate, as the sounding box. Looking again at the story which began with LaVonne on St. Fursey Lake and her husband Vern losing his job at the nerve-gas lab, and LeRoy with his missing dog, here is the material for the sounding box:

The beauty of a Minnesota lake

The fragility of a Minnesota lake (ecologically)

The desperate evil of manufacturing nerve-gas—an industry that employs some nice people like Vern

The simple griefs of a simple person who loves nature (LeRoy)

And the simple griefs of animals (Silver)

Because all things in the universe are at least somehow linked, we look for linkage. We are looking for a subplot which will twine with and serve the main story. All of these characters— even LaVonne—love nature. It is their dignity. Some of these characters are ethically unconscious—perhaps LeRoy, certainly Silver. One is ethically aware: Vern.

That's enough for Chekhov right there. It is a problem to get LeRoy somehow to bump into Vern during the course of the day and to get Vern sooner or later either back north to LaVonne or not. If Vern at the last minute, when he is already in the town of St. Fursey, remembers he needs oil for the Evinrude, he might stop back at the station where LeRoy is looking depressed. Vern is feeling depressed now, too. The elation of having made a sacrificial stand for his values wore off as he drove up Interstate 35E. He speaks kindly to LeRoy, finds out about the dog, and offers to take LeRoy, when he gets off, for a drink at the VFW. There starts the conversation we have already breezed through. After LeRoy unwisely slugs someone, Vern quickly gets him out. He is back to LaVonne very late, and now he is fragrant with whisky. The story can stop short of their meeting, or it can have their meeting as a denouement. Perhaps he tells her about quitting his job: he has never discussed the nerve-gas before.

Up until now, LaVonne has been the villain of this story. Maybe she listens to him instead of upbraiding him about losing the job. When he describes how the little animals writhe and scream in their part of the lab, she shudders—and then, in a rare moment of confiding, tells him how she felt when she first helped her parents and Dieter, their old hired hand, cut off the heads of leghorns. The headless chickens rhumbaed around the farmyard to get "a good bleed." LaVonne kept thinking she could put the heads back on. She thought she could stop the evil. But both her father and mother had a good sense of humor, and they taught her to laugh at herself. And the hired hand, Dieter, grinned and said, "If you can't deal with killing chickens, there's going to be a lot you can't deal with!" Her father put his work-worn, generous, warm hand around the back of her neck. At that time, she was such a little thing his fingers nearly met at the front.

CHAPTER THREE: NOTES

1. Donald Attwater, *The Penguin Dictionary of Saints*, Penguin Books, Harmondsworth, 1965, p. 165.

2. The following leaders, collectively, have persecuted and murdered many times the number of victims of the Nazi Holocaust. Each of these leaders received weapons, training, money, and/or military support from the United States: Chiang (China), Thieu (Vietnam), Ky (Vietnam), Sukarno (Indonesia), Pol Pot (Cambodia), Marcos (the Phillipines), Mugabe (Zaire), Idi Amin (Uganda), Savimbi (Angola), "The Generals" (Argentina), "The Generals" (Brazil), "The Junta" (Greece), Eric Gairy (Grenada), The Shah (Iran), The Ayatollah (Iran), Pinochet (Chile), Begin, Sharon, Peres, Shamir (Israel), Noriega (Panama), Batista (Cuba), Papa Doc, Baby Doc, Namphy (Haiti), Somoza (Nicaragua), Arena Party (El Salvador), Rios Mont (Guatemala), Sadat (Egypt), Trujillo (Dominican Republic), Deng (China), Rabukah (Fiji), Vang Pao (Laos), Rhee, KCIA (South Korea).This list is provided by Mary Shepherd, writing in the newsletter of Women Against Military Madness, WAMM, Vol. 8, No. 6, February, 1990, p. 7.

In an article entitled "U.S. Aided '65 Massacre of Indonesian Left," *The Boston Globe*, May 23, 1990, Kathy Kadane reports that "for the first time, American officials have acknowledged that in 1965 they systematically compiled comprehensive lists of Communist operatives, from the top echelons down to village cadres. As many as 5,000 names were furnished to the army, and the Americans later checked off the names of those who had been killed or captured, according to U.S. officials."

Because of our comparatively free press in the United States, educated Americans know about our foreign policy. I will make what I suspect is a conservative guess—that 450,000 educated, alert Americans feel some misery about American foreign policy from time to time.

3. Michael True, "Postmodernist Poetry in General—And Brother Antoninus in Particular," *Cross-Currents*, Vol. 34, Fall 1989, p. 360.

CHAPTER FOUR

The People

Characters Made in the Usual Way

It is important to remember: deliberate technique is only for drafts *after* the first complete one. No one should be thinking of *how* for the first draft: technical thinking spoils the inventive theme-giving ambiance.

There are two broad aspects to making the people of a story: one can build characters the way journalists and extroverts do. You look at a person, a real one or an imagined one, and looking at him or her *from the outside*, you observe the person as carefully as you can, noticing everything. Here's a short checklist for human beings. All humans have a secret or public list of values, conscious or unconscious:

Work: they know how to do or want to do or used to do

Love: people they love or fail to love. It is a love life, even if it is an empty love life

Hobbies: good or inane or wicked

A past

A future

Intense wanting of something or hoping for something— or none: flaccid ideals, a bland contentment

A secret character—some notions or qualities they don't exhibit

A public facade (or none)

A whole set of weaknesses or strengths

The ability (or none) to be inspired

Looks. The millions of ways human beings or animals look

Two examples of characters who could have been drawn up with the above list resting on their authors' desks are Katherine Mansfield's Bertha Young in "Bliss" and D.H. Lawrence's mother of Paul in "The Rocking-Horse Winner."

Even if one never used a tenth of the list above in a story, it is not a bad idea to know those aspects of a character. The author needs to know everything: it prevents literary hanky-panky—that is, making up a stereotype, for example, then giving it unusual dialogue to bring it to life.

A second reason to make sure you know so much about characters is psychological: knowledge makes affection, and new affection makes it easier to leave old affection (one's life). Many highly civilized adults *simply lack affection* for what is unknown to them. (In *Emma*, Mr. Knightly, that pontificating fellow who was perfect in all things, was irritated with Emma because she was so ignorant of the physical work, "the honorable work" of farming, that she lighthandedly tried to lift Harriet out of the class of a would-be farmer's wife. Emma didn't know *any* work, in fact, and therefore was unaffectionate.)

Here is a surprising bit of normal psychology: people feel more disdain than they suppose they feel. We don't notice it in everyday life, but it immediately shows up in our fiction unless we recognize and confront it. As with other common human failings, one blames oneself, thinking one is the only person hobbled with such and such a weakness: I thought I was the only person trying to write stories who seemed to slight so many of the characters. I was horrified when a first-rate editor told me to cut out the scorn and cut it out straight off. Years later, I was making up some exercises for the COMPAS Literary Post. The Literary Post, sponsored by St. Paul, Minnesota's COMPAS, a multi-faceted arts planning and community service organization, was a project founded in 1980 to serve elder Minnesotans by mail. Any state resident over sixty might send manuscripts to a professional writer, who would assist in the writing and maintain a correspondence with the participant. In the first year, fifty-four people participated. In the second, seven hundred applied: I worked with about two hundred. Since then, it has taken five writers a year to handle all the participants. The shining good of the COMPAS Literary Post is that old people in remote areas can be in touch with writers who take their work seriously. I found a good pen-and-ink drawing of a 1930s radio. I attached it to a writing exercise. The writers were to describe a radio program which they themselves didn't happen to like but which some character (a friend, neighbor or relation) did: they were to explain *how* that character enjoyed the program. The last sentences of the exercise read: "How, *exactly*, does the person enjoy the program? See if you can write about it without letting even a half-inch of disdain filter into what you say."

I was astonished. No one could do the exercise. First, no one chose to describe an enjoyment more cultured or more elegant or braver than their own: no one chose a character who listened for the likenesses between Brahms and early Dvorák. No one chose someone who was able to watch and think over exposures of harsh American manipulations in Vietnam and Laos. *Everyone* chose to describe

a person of lesser education;

a person who liked fantasy and glitz better than reality (soaps);

a person who watched not just Vikings, but Steelers, Skins, '49ers, even Seahawks.

Most of the writers added a little conventional wisdom at the end: "I fail to see what so and so gets out of that program, but, of course, backgrounds and tastes vary." They couldn't keep off it.

The true exercise was a revision in which the writer might not settle for "failing to see what they got out of it": you had humbly to imagine what they got out of it. It was a very writerly exercise. It led me to realize I was not the only person cursed with kneejerk disdain, but that it is an occupational problem of *writers*, generally. It led me to hypothesize how that disdain gets so prevalent, and how to get rid of it (discussed in the Introduction).

If we find ourselves writing in someone towards whom we feel faintly mocking, it is a good idea to check through the list for that person and give the person a little something for which you the author can respect him or her. A hobby say, of organic flower and vegetable planting. On second thought, perhaps not: organic virtue is a cliché now. I am longing for a marvelous, brave, spirited, witty woman character to be the hero of an 800-page work of art—a woman who has this one peculiarity: she hates vegetarians. She can smell that old, boiled brown-rice smell one-hundred yards off. She can spot soy milk from across the room. Otherwise, she is a wonderful person. More seriously: if you are describing a person who easily obeys orders, taking pride in prompt obedience instead of in judging for himself or herself whether the order is just or not, you may need some balancing benignancy so you haven't just set up the person to be knocked down.

It is not always necessary to feel affectionate towards a character, but it is always necessary to be interested. For example, say that you want a character who tortured or murdered helpless civilians during World War II. I bring this up because the men who did that—Nazis—are by the hundreds still among us; there are hundreds of them now in their late sixties through early nineties, undiscovered, living ordinary lives. It is ridiculous to try to feel affectionate towards such people in literature: it is no good giving them some "balancing" virtues. What you can do is show such a person working away at some intricate project. You need technical know-how of that project, because the details you give must be fresh, not picked out of the collective information we all have. Here is a rough example:

> The two men stood awkwardly at the edge of the forest pond. LaVonne's dad had leapt off the 3120 when he saw old Dieter bring up the pick-up. "What'd they say about the strawberries?" he asked right away.
>
> "Good luck!" Dieter said. "Good news! It's not Red Steel. It's water rot, though. All the Sparklers have it. Some of the Midways."
>
> He got out of the truck, and the two of them hovered in one of the rows. It was always a surprise that strawberry plants *look* so healthy even when they are frighteningly sick. "The cure," Dieter said, "is total water control. You have the forest pond, so you're in luck. All you have to do now is resurvey and get all the plants onto ridges and then irrigate, irrigate, irrigate."
>
> The owner of the farm was now sixty, with a whole household to consider. "What a job," he said quietly.
>
> They had ambled over to the pond. It was late afternoon, and cooling. They looked down at the black water. Stacked beside it were the aluminum-pipe sections which they had to move out each spring and restack each fall.
>
> "All that work," the poor fellow said.
>
> "O yes," Dieter said, "But you've got me. I am an old hand at setting up water systems."
>
> "Ja," the younger man said smiling. "You were irrigating at the time of the Flood. Don't tell me."

That is an extraordinarily dull passage of fiction, but it enables a writer to present an old Nazi who has a helpful, technical skill, without sentimentalizing him. The usual way to present old Nazis is to have them be very good with children—making doll houses, that activity so dear to Nordics. If you look through short stories that are beautiful, you can find how the author handled the despicable people in them: in Mark Helprin's great story "The Schreuderspitze," a nasty commercial photographer named Franzen, who disdains the spiritually inclined hero of the story, explains how he defeated the hero in winning a bid from a turbine company.[1] He explains in detail how he faked an interest in turbines so the company would think they were getting a very committed man. Helprin is able to keep our attention on a ghastly, commercial-minded and uncharitable sort of person because of the exact *particulars* of the fellow's marketing strategy.

Characters Made Out of Our Various Selves

The second major way of character-making is putting a cast of characters together made up of your own various selves. It isn't a complicated idea. It uses a psychotherapeutic process in which you hear out what a character is concerned with, make sure you have it right, ask enough questions of the character so you know his or her *feelings* about the situation. And then make some guesses about what *meaning* the situation has for that character. The process is called empathy: it characteristically is done by

1. Listening

2. Asking for more data, or for clarification on anything unclear

3. Reflecting back the data

4. Asking or listening for the feeling

5. Reflecting back the feeling

6. Asking or guessing or listening for the meaning

7. Reflecting back the meaning

In order to do this in real life, the therapist or skilled psychologist and the client sit opposite each other. In literature, we have only the author and the character (who isn't actual), so the author must pretend to be the character and answer the questions. Of course, one doesn't go through such an elaborate, deliberate procedure as the empathy program above each time—but it is a first-rate model. Authors can use parts of it. It works because it makes us inwardly part of one another: we can speak for one another. Tolstoy is so wonderful at guessing about how others feel. Many men have tried to describe how a pretty woman feels when she enters the ballroom: Tolstoy gets just *one detail* absolutely right, and we see her and become her and we care what happens to her: it is all because Tolstoy, using his imagination, figured out that for Kitty, high heels actually made her feel lighter and nearer dancing—they *eased* her, rather than hobbling her. Now that is true of high heels about one-tenth of the time. Mostly, if you walk from 50th street in Manhattan either across one block or down three in high heels, the mindless discomfort of it drives you to bad temper—all for what—for the two panhandlers? the one potential mugger? the ninety-six other strangers passed along the way? or for the cellar windows not so dirty but that they reflect your ankles flashing, broken, of course, by the iron burglary-prevention bars? But for that one-tenth of the time, Tolstoy had it right. He was right about Kitty. Tolstoy is one of the greatest character-makers-through-guesswork of all time: we have his common soldiery, his young officers' delight in being able to hand around goodies to tentmates, Napoleon's infinite satisfaction in Prince Andrei's being so severely wounded. Tolstoy periodically wanted, dreadfully sometimes, absent-mindedly at still other times, to find human beings part and parcel of one another: that particular spiritual stance gave him his merciful imagination. A part of him was young girl dancing, and a part was sixteen-year-old Petya at the moment of his ridiculous charge against the French and a moment later, his death.

Sometimes, dividing oneself up into separate characters is like the Jungian psychological process called "Active Imagination" in which one deliberately has a conversation between one's ordinary self and some other voice in oneself. As mentioned earlier, therapists use it to help people see how torn they are between the various motivations inside themselves. It is an awfully good way to make a character come real—for some people. I won't speak of it further because I don't use it myself.

Sometimes, when we are setting a scene, it is useful to put in a blank character, the way electricians put in extra circuitry. If you have a little scene with two people in it whom you know you want to have in it—let's say a father and his daughter—add a third person without a face, sex, or name. As you imagine the scene, let this third person accompany the others. You may suddenly find a point of view you would like shown in the scene—which neither the father nor the daughter could logically express. Then put the third person to work.

A father and daughter and S.E. (Someone Else) were told to start walking from the north end of the cornfield southward. There were ten or eleven hunters in all, everyone arranged about twelve or thirteen cornrows apart. The corn, which had been picked but not yet disced and plowed, kept touching their knees with its broken stalks. Their feet tromped on the woody fibers, the sculpted grey leaves, and now and then struck a stiff cob of "down corn" the picker had missed.

The daughter, rather used to hunting weekends, kept an unpleasant, rather fierce expression on her face. Her father had gained weight now he was old: he was doing this only to be obliging, and he carried his .12 gauge leisurely in the crook of his elbow. He wanted to show himself to Donny as a pleasant father-in-law. He wanted Kate to find him an easy man to invite for a weekend. Frankly, he supposed, he wanted to be invited much more than he was. He flopped along in his old Sorels. A rabbit flashed by.

"Get that, Dad!" cried the young married woman.

He felt a flash of misery: he could tell—he felt it—from the way she barked the order, "Get that!" that she was not happily married after all. She was keeping herself hard—perhaps to protect herself from a vicious husband. He wasn't sure. He didn't want to think about it, either. He wanted to go on thinking Donny wasn't all that bright but had a hearty, amiable temperament.

Aloud he called, "Ah, Katie! That nice, furry warm rabbit!" He said it in a genial shout, but the third member of their party then lurched across the smashed rows of corn, leaving his own row to come join them at a trot.

"Hey! I left that rabbit for you! What's going on?" he snapped—but in the next second, he gave his glittering smile.

"O—" the daughter said, smiling fast, "We left it for *you*!"

The father thought, she already lies to him. He already has a foul temper. She is afraid of him. His heart felt as if it bulged and went to iron on him. If it were a thousand years ago, he thought, I'd just shoot him. He had some idea that in the middle-ages you could do anything that needed doing without trouble from the cops, it was so far back . . . .

In that passage, the S.E. (Someone Else) became the young woman's husband. In any case, if the third figure doesn't do you any good after a draft or two, you can take it out.

One's own Values Listing is useful for making characters because our imaginations hate picturing virtues, vices, hopes, or fears which we don't experience ourselves. We can imagine our own very well—even if they are old ones we no longer care for. We can remember them and recover a few virtues or vices from the past from this or that character. An old value I no longer care for: religious excitement. I spent three years of my life hanging about with people who were what was in the late sixties and early seventies called "in the Spirit." Most spoke in tongues or said they did. Some could heal (only one whom I knew, but he really did heal people for about four or five years before the gift disappeared as suddenly as it had come to him). I hung about with those people because although they were not brighter than others, they had a holy view of things: knowing them was like living in nature, although we were all living in a city. The morning seemed mysterious to me. The evenings seemed holy. I read dozens of books about spiritual life. Even at that time, however, I noticed that the Born Again people and the in-the-Spirit people were mostly people who had lived purely commercial or mass-culture lives before: they were housewives with a sharp eye for bargains, who fed their children their meals at aluminum-tube furniture, often speaking disrespectfully of the children in their presence ("What kids don't say, huh?") and several of the men who had written books about their conversions said that Jesus had helped them to increase their sales percentages. I noticed those people and a part of me, a voice which at least posed as commonsensical, said that sudden conversion was the property of knaves, an emotion as suspect as patriotism ("the last refuge of a scoundrel") and nostalgia. Nostalgia is the emotion people feel who are heartless with earth, air, plants, animals and other people. You have but to murmur, "Now when you were a kid . . . " and their eyes fill nearly immediately. The greatest brutes of them swivel their gaze to the window, look outward, and you see that shining eye and the raised chin, and you think, the human male or the human female has got something *fine* about it after all. Nostalgia is one of the most decorative of feelings.

All this to say one of my old, no-longer-current values is religious-conversion feelings. The memory is useful, because I have *been* there and can recall the particulars.

Here is how such a recalled old value might come in useful. Let us say we want the short story to have these three characters in it: Peter, Natalie, and John. All we know about them is that they are now having drinks and soon they will have dinner. Peter and John are colleagues in some high-level government or private-sector project. Natalie is Peter's wife. For the purposes of the story,

> Natalie is furious at Peter and is drinking too much;
>
> Peter is being gentle about her bad behavior (she is jeering);
>
> John says little: he is in his miserable thoughts, wishing that Peter would get "some help" for Natalie.

Now we add to that:

> All three of them are First World people who majored in one or another of the humanities, each of them worth about $78,000 a year.

If we ask a very good question of each story character—What would they be doing if they were not doing what they *are* doing?—we feel behind us and them a great vague shadow of things other. By saying all three are *First World*, we wake up consciousness of Third World. By asking "What would any of them be doing if they were not doing this—having drinks before dinner?'' we ask about the whole species, and specifically we ask about their lives secret or unrecognized in themselves.

Let's say John is the enlightened one of this lot: he has two qualities which don't always accompany one another in the same person. He is psychologically awake, and he has good manners. The good manners in him make him go up to Peter and say, "Peter you're looking awfully anxious! Can I get you anything?'' The psychological perspicacity in him would ask, "Peter, you are looking awfully anxious! What damned thing has happened?'' Tonight, because Natalie is there and they need to get through the evening somehow (a waiter has taken their order and will come fetch them from the sitting rooms when their whitefish is ready), John drops psychology and goes with manners. We don't know what the conversation will be: we don't even know if the conversation will take place here where we started, in the clubhouse: as Lewis Thomas says of basic research, we work in an atmosphere of probable failure, humor, unsureness.

Natalie is a tremendously hostile, neurotic woman who spoils the evening not just this evening, but nearly every time. They have been married twelve or thirteen years. After one drink, she begins revealing all sorts of unpleasant personal data (which data we will think up in particular in some later draft). She makes one hostile remark to Peter and slurs about him in a carrying tone. Everyone (for there are three other sofa-arrangements in the sitting room of the club) is horrified, but this is the twentieth century, not the nineteenth, so they don't mutter, "My word, why doesn't that poor man have a sharp word with his wife! Someone needs to lay down the law to that woman!''

Instead, in the office the next day, someone—John, the man at dinner tonight—says: "Good God, Peter, haven't you thought of getting some professional help for your wife? Don't you see she is just *crying out* for help?''

Peter regards John gravely. He doesn't take offense because he has been told that gentlemen don't take offense where none is intended: "Actually, Natalie is making wonderful progress! We're getting on top of this thing! She's ever so much better!''

Peter gets up from his desk then and walks quietly over to the window. He seems to be looking very far out of it, with his chin raised, his hands clasped behind him, like a responsible soldier at Parade Rest. His whole body, as we see it in dark profile before the bright out-of-doors, gives off the tone of a captain trying to think through the troubles of his soldiers—giving them his best, most personal attention.

John says, "You're good about it, Peter."

"Nuts!" Peter says in an attractive, no-nonsense tone. "Now," he says, "Enough of the personal. Let's get through some of this god-awful mess on my desk. I've looked over your suggestions for the top spots. I think they're terrific. Any reason we can't go with what you came up with, Jack? I *think* I like everything you came in with."

Both men draw their chairs around his desk. John keeps glancing at Peter with admiration.

It isn't much of a scene, but is a beginning of a story. It has neither more nor less promising material in it than any other *donnée* of the ordinary, realistic sort. It has some shadowy possibilities. For one thing, this Peter thinks he is God with his attractive, grave, courteous, ghastly patronizing. How superior he is! How calculated the *persona* he affects! How much he wants us to admire his decency! If we use the journalist's way of describing character, we easily make his well-cut suit, his neat hair, his clear forehead. If we look inward, and split our own soul in two so we can have a conversation about him and ask some questions, we ask, "Do you want people to admire you, Peter?" "Yes. And so they should." Let us keep asking. "Do you want your wife to behave badly the way she does? You pretend you don't and are being long-suffering—but the truth is?" He agrees that he wants his wife's bad behavior. After all, he does not ask her to see a psychotherapist, does he? He does not go to marriage counseling because that would be a very non-prep-school blight on his own escutcheon. We ask him, "What are you 'on top of,'" then? You told John you were getting 'on top of this.' What's the 'this?' " No answer. "Peter," we say, "when we just asked you that question about psychology, you turned away and looked out the window, not at us. You showed us your back, dark, silhouetted in the light from the window. Do you always choose to look *out*, rather than *in?*"

He draws himself up.

Peter Tenebray's name reminds me that he's a man with a shadow like anyone else. Symbolic names did something for readers in Dickens's time; they don't now, but they help the author while the story is in progress. I wrote an old woman character who came along better once I had named her Svea Istava, Finnish for faithful friend. It is an Author's Help, so to speak.

If there is something not-so-good about Peter as he wishes to appear or as he seems to John, we can start trying things, like having him involved in some dreadful other activity. During the day he works for the C.I.A. or he is a lawyer for some company making more acid rain than all the others together—etc. It's a good idea to throw out the first ideas you have at any time. Maybe it is some secret life of John's or Natalie's, not of Peter's, which will shed light on Peter and on all of them.

Checking through my Values Listing, including old values once held no longer loved, I find religious conversion feelings. Good—let Natalie be an eager prayer-group member.

That's the *first* thing I thought of. Following the old rule, "That's the *first* thing you thought of, what's the *second?*" I say, no, she is not a religious enthusiast. She is the only one in the room of Born Agains who is not. She has tried but is going to leave the group. Why would she leave the group? It is time to split ourselves into two with our ordinary self as one and this time Natalie as the second voice. "Why'd you leave the group, Natalie?" "Because," she says instantly, "They are phonies, too." "All of them?" "No—the leaders. They pretend to be so—so—*good!* But in fact, what they are doing is . . . "

Then we have to think: what is an evil which human beings do?

I won't carry this further. The idea was to show how rather dead, center-stage, a story plot can be. One of the best stories ever written, "Gooseberries," by Chekhov, has the most dismal plot.[2] Two people walking get caught in a rain; they walk across a wet field to find the country place of a man one of them knows. They bathe. They go into the house where a beautiful young woman waits on them. One of them tells a story about a brother who wanted nothing in life so much as to own a gooseberry farm; he married an old woman for her money, starved her to death, to pay for the gooseberry farm. *That* is the plot. It doesn't start off any more auspiciously than our evening with John, Natalie, and Peter.

Questions to Ask of the Characters

Some lists of one's own of questions to ask the characters can make a mere *donnée* into something which becomes story. Having lists seems rigid and formulaic, because it is. Like formulae, lists serve very specific uses: they protect us from writing stories which nowhere touch on our true feelings or the issues we care for. They keep the tone *up*. This is especially important for American writers, because hour after hour we hear so many junk-values and so much junk-language around us.

I wasn't alive in the 1880s to the 1930s when the psychological forces working *against* art were different from those against art now: then, as now, the usual victims of arrogance— women, the poor, and anyone not white—could scarcely get anything said. What we have now is disparagement of Gentle Feeling. Kindliness, although still practiced, has gone a little underground. Most of our short stories are centered on fairly vicious material:

Careerism

Violence and crime

Adultery and treachery

Self-centered sexuality

If such a generalization sounds absurd, try deliberately listening for the word "just" in its sense of meaning "only", and you will see that people are shuttering the windows of their ideas with this "just." I guess that's just me (ignorant): it is just an idea I had (privilege). I guess I was "just wondering, is all." Once you start hearing self-deprecatory remarks, you can start listening for which kinds of subjects are receiving that timid, wavery disrespect. Usually it is the idealistic subjects. If simple, good feelings weren't out of style, we wouldn't hear the apologetic tone. Roughly speaking (I am writing with the principle that one accurate no-nonsense generalization is worth eight flaccid caveats)—roughly speaking, we spend our time exercising those powers we have and exercising as much mercy towards powerless victims as we decide we have time for. Writers write both for affection for life as it is and from an indignation. (I am leaving out of this discussion those who will say anything which the market suggests will be profitable. There are always hacks; there is always a little sleazy inclination to hack inside us, to fall back on *shtick*—but so long as we recognize it, we needn't discuss it further.)

There is another presence that brings down American literature a little: it is a mild, socially acceptable cynicism. When serious authors let themselves do genre writing, it says to young writers, why be serious?

I bring all this up because if a story made of Natalie, Peter, and John, and such few others as we may add, is to make any tie to our hearts' truths, we shall have to think: is cynicism all right or not? Ivan Ilyich did no particular harm. Shall we take harm seriously? We can have the noble-appearing Peter engaging in something dreadful at the same time as he poses as an even-tempered husband. Shall we have John constantly suggesting to Peter that he and his wife get counseling, and then we follow John home to where some appalling thing is taking place? Shall we let Peter be contractor for a nerve-gas lab?

Management of Characters

I am going to lay down some guidelines for managing the characters of a short story. Lest such an idea—management, of all things!—offend, here is why I feel so strongly about it. I went to a good school which happened to have as its acting dean my senior year a first-rate teacher of creative writing. Alice Sweeney gave me two gifts as a writer: she said a) become a writer. You can. And b) she returned an essay I had handed in with marginal questions—not marginal comments—but marginal *questions*. "What exactly is happening here?" she asked. "Would he have felt that and then said that?" she asked. The essay—or rather, a simple piece of autobiography since I had no particular idea in mind—was about listening to Tchaikovsky's First Piano Concerto—only the first movement of it, over and over, with my brother Malcolm. "Did Malcolm do that?" she asked. "What was he thinking?" she asked.

Alice Sweeney showed me that I needed to be *generating*, not organizing, material throughout at least another draft. I made another draft. That hardworking teacher had as her principal job getting all of us greedy little beasts into Ivy League colleges (hard to do in the fall of 1946 and winter of 1947 because men were coming back from World War II, using the wonderful G.I. Bill). She kindly read three more versions of my Tchaikovsky piece. Rewriting changed my life, because it made me a reviser. Revision, as we are constantly told, is the secret of literature.

Then, with my family's faith in the seven sisters, I went to Wellesley, where *no teacher during my four years there* knew how to write fiction. There was a fiction teacher, but she did not write well herself, and her idea was at the level of Writer's Magazine: write to sell to certain markets. There was a fine writer named Mary Doyle Curran, author of an autobiographical novel about lace-curtain and shanty-Irish people in the Boston area, but she wasn't interested in fiction in which there are *several* characters: she was interested in the chronology of her own life.[3]

During my four years in college, I learned nothing about how to write fiction. At Harvard, not thirty miles away, several teachers showed their students how to *present* (show) rather than *describe* (tell about) characters, how to follow *tone* throughout a work, how to ask questions of the manuscript. I am still cross that I wasn't given the information on how the short story is made. I had only on-the-job learning, which is slower than theory.

Here are some procedures, therefore, to speed the invisible spirit into its gaudy shapes of character and words. Please absolutely remember that *none of these methods* should be even lightly looked at until the first draft of a story or of something—what Hampl calls "a piece of writing" perhaps—is done through to what may be the end.

First question to ask the manuscript: are there enough characters? Make a list of everyone in the story so far. Make a list of all the settings. You don't need events at this point, only settings. Are there enough people? If not, add some now. We fiction writers are all skilled liars in any case: simply grab some relations or neighbors or acquaintances of some kind, and stick them arbitrarily somewhere into the story fabric.

Now: second question: are there too many characters? During the first, generative draft or drafts you may have put too many relations, hybrid relations-cum-acquaintances and invented folk into the story. A short story is not a novel: everyone in it is slightly symbolic. Because there is so little space every object or person counts for a good deal. Just as in a flag: if there are already fifty stars in it, no one will likely object if you tuck in an extra four or five. If there was one star in it, as in the Romanian flag, one notices when it is cut out.

If there are too many characters, you can combine some. Looking at the two partial, irresolute stories we've discussed so far:

1. The narrative about LaVonne, Vern, and LeRoy (slight mention of Vern's mother and of a girl LeRoy once liked)

2. The narrative about Peter, John and Natalie, and Natalie's parents, earlier

If we had in our first complete draft the names of all the people drinking at the VFW with LeRoy, some would need to go. Without wrecking the plot, it would be handy to keep Vern's meeting with LeRoy.

We can try expanding a scene. Here are LeRoy and Vern again . . . just a try, the way geometers try . . .

"Silver," LeRoy said. "Some bastard stole Silver. . . ." He kept skillfully dragging the squeegee across Vern's windshield.

"When do you get off?" Vern said.

"Not till five."

"I'll buy you at the V.F." Vern said. "Hey, LeRoy, put some cans of 2-cycle oil in the trunk."

They wander over to the VFW after a while. Vern has a key. Vern and LeRoy tuck themselves into a booth with some others. Here we need to boil down the group—perhaps to two people—maybe a man and his wife—the wife keeping up drink for drink with the man. She has a habit of laying her hand on his arm whenever he raises his glass. (What is that? I've noticed that a hundred times if I've noticed it once: someone's wife puts her hand on his arm: it is to control him. . . . My guess is, after he gets filthy drunk—and let us say this one in the story is going to get filthy drunk—he and she go home, and perhaps he is abusive. She knows that's coming, and she won't be able to handle him then. But that's not now. For now, they are happy together. This is the best time of their marriage—sauced at the VF.) We are inside her, now, a little drunk. Someone tomorrow will ask, "What did you do last night, Kate?" "Hell, Don and I got like totally juiced with two weird guys there, this well-dressed one I've seen around, summer people, Vern someone, and then Beske from the 76 station. I want to tell you my Don was cold sober compared to them guys. We had fun." As she was talking jubilantly on the phone, rain pounding down, thank God after all this drought all the time, she remembered that when Don and she got home, the Champ lolling from side to side of the road, she'd put her foot down the way she'd been promising herself she would, damn it not tonight, she said, all the time they were at the VF, she putting her hand on his arm—having fun with Don—he was fun when he was in the VF and he was twice the man of those fruitfronts like that LeRoy Beske who was crying of all darn things. Not tonight, she had promised herself; but when they got home, he said, Into bed, little lady, fast, too, so you don't catch one on your butt, and she remembered like cold silver how for six weeks Doc kept her jaw wired shut and Donny would laugh and say, you don't look bad wired shut and you don't *sound bad either*—you can't even answer now, can you? She remembered that, and with a kind of perfect hatred, she undressed so he could violate her without getting so mad he hit her in the face. On the phone, she said, "We need the rain."

Anyway, all that passes through Kate's mind—Bertha's mind, Estelle's mind, Verona's mind, Mercein's mind, Carol's mind—try the names around a little. We can put her in the story for a draft or two, her and Donny the beater, because they're part of the life of St. Fursey the town, and the husband, Donny, gives us someone who will insult the slough and the DNR and the environmentalists, so that LeRoy, a mechanic with a short reach and no hostile instincts, who is drunk *only* because someone stole his Lab—LeRoy can slug Donny good—across the table—the table shining like St. Fursey Lake. Then this kind of eleganzo from The Cities, Vern, gets LeRoy out of there before Donny puts him out for six hours—it helps that Donny's wife has her hand on Donny's arm. First we wanted it for realism: now it helps the plot. She has (Vern wouldn't know this, and later we must sort out the point of view) a stake in not letting Don hit anyone while they're at the VF: if he does, he gets into the mode of hitting people; then he will beat her up a lot—like five or six minutes all over her face—instead of just raping her. So she will slow Donny's arm if she can. She will slow down Donny's huge, careful, lionlike rise to his feet: she presses her hand, with its four fat pads of fingers, on his plaid shirtsleeve—it gives Vern the minute or so he needs to get LeRoy out.

What is going on for Vern? He feels heroic: he is going to take his own grief—loss of job out of principle—and transform it into kindness to this LeRoy. Vern is not self-deceptive, however. He says to the posey, virtuous side of himself, Don't try that on. You know perfectly well that yes, you are doing something nice for LeRoy, but only because you are scared to go home to LaVonne because you haven't got an anniversary present and she wanted the Evinrude greased.

He gets drunk, too. What a mean-minded woman I am married to! he thinks. The liquor makes the idea seem very fresh to him; he is quite convinced he has not thought that thought dozens of times before.

If we make a character list, we now have

LeRoy

Vern

LaVonne

Don the beater

Kate his wife

and, of course, others—whom we needn't bother about any more than Shakespeare bothered about those servants and soldiers who did the "alarums."

Sometimes there are others we ought to take a passing look at. We know LaVonne is squinting across the lake. What's on the other side of the lake? If we glance again at the check-list of issues which give vibration and depth of sound to the violin strings of the plot:

The beauty of a Minnesota lake,

The fragility of a Minnesota lake,

The desperate evil of nerve gas,

The desperate custom of nice people taking jobs with companies or universities which have taken evil contracts for evil products, and

The past of the *place*, its future, the people living around there.

It crosses my mind that Vern is now without a job. Perhaps there are other unemployed people—all the plywood-company layoffs across the lake? What if it was LaVonne's dream—all her life—not to be tied to a man who gets periodically laid off? Maybe she is from the east end of St. Fursey, where the plywood-plant people live—and on purpose she married Vern, who is summer folks.

Now—he comes back on their 10th anniversary (5th anniversary? 25th anniversary? We can decide later). It is 9 p.m. He tells her that *he* is fired. She married Vern for his *class* not for his *principles* (whatever they are). Classy people keep their jobs, she had thought. Not this clown she married.

Wrestling with this issue: is LaVonne too awful? If spirit lives in each of us, is there anything a little redemptive in her?

What we are considering at this point is which characters are needed for the story. We started with LaVonne, but maybe she is not needed at all.

Maybe the story starts with a man taking a black Lab out of the trunk or the backseat of his car and urging it to go with him, but it holds back. He says to it, "Well, you don't know me now—but you'll learn to know me. You're just a dog. So you had one master. Now you got another. What is all the shit about? Listen, you black Lab bitch—life is *full* of shit, I got news for you."

Walter Scott would start the story like that. Dickens would start a chapter like that—with minor characters who influence the plot in a palpable way. They cross a field and find a body. Or they are graverobbers so they know when a coffin is empty and when it's not, having dug the hole for nothing. Chekhov would never introduce a figure just for exposition. If the figure said, Life is full of shit, Chekhov might bring the man in—but if he did, he would take him seriously as a character: he would show him in perspective as he does other characters.

If we don't want casually to bring in another person, is there any character already with us whom we could have steal the dog? First thought: Donny, of course, the bad fellow who beats his wife. He would steal a dog. But that is the *first thing we thought of: what is the second*? Donny would *not* steal a dog. He is a Missouri Synod Lutheran churchgoer—honest as the day is long, not, as he would snarl, like one of them druggies at the east end of St. Fursey Lake. Might Kate steal the dog? If her and Don's daughter finally ran away after Donny called her a whore for getting pregnant, would she want something to love? Would she think it didn't belong to someone? No—it had a collar and tag. Not Kate.

Would LaVonne steal a dog? If no one would steal the dog, shall we cut the dog-stealing?

We can leave the problem: that story is not really our story. It is only an example of the kinds of questions to ask, before we settle upon a cast of characters.

Three Appearances of Each Character by Mention at Least

This is a unifying technique. Bring in each character by mention or in the action at least three times, making sure that they are mentioned or introduced *early in the story*. These two considerations are vital. A short story cannot be shapeless or all theatricality is lost. We have all had the disappointment of ghost stories carelessly told in camp in which the teller introduces new characters late, because he or she forgot to get them in earlier: "Just then a lion came by. Oh yeah, I forgot to tell you, someone had busted into the zoo that same night and let a lion out. Well, anyway, this lion came by just then and . . . " That is a tale told by an amateur.

We can start by reading through the manuscript, with the now-typed list of characters we've decided on, on our desk, beside the manuscript. Any characters introduced into the first draft late can be dropped in earlier, at least by mention. A story is a perfect skein, a planned work of art. That means that we don't read on page 20 of its 23 pages:

> Well, then a distant cousin showed up, and LeRoy inherited $400 with which he was able to buy not one but two purebred black Lab puppies.

We can have the distant cousin and the inheritance if we like, but if we do, we must drop off casually, early in the story, that LeRoy had a distant cousin.

Say that the story now has this chronology:

1. Vern is with his boss in the Twin Cities (the nerve-gas lab).

2. The boss fires him. Vern drives to St. Fursey, Minnesota.

3. He stops and talks to LeRoy at the 76 station.

4. Vern and LeRoy get drunk with Don and Kate and others at the VFW.

5. Vern finally makes it home to LaVonne who then tells him, all her life the one thing she counted on was he wouldn't get laid off like an ordinary workman and now look.

6. They sit on the dock and look at the acid-rain-affected White Spruces across the lake. They imagine the day there won't be any trees. There will be this desert in Iowa. The Great Iowa desert it will be called. Minnesota will be some kind of hot grasslands. The conifers will have marched, a half-mile a year, up into northern Ontario.

A dreary set of scenes—but we can let it ride for the moment, like a geometric hypothesis. If some of it has no heart, we drop it. We insert into #4:

> Somewhere in the conversation at the VF, before it got ugly, Vern tells Kate, "You look like my cousin." He wants to say something nice. Kate looks pleased. She usually isn't in the conversation at all except to say, "Gee, Don—no politics or religion, remember? Remember, honey? No politics, hey? No religion?"
> LeRoy gave a harsh laugh, "Be glad you don't look like my cousin! She may be a rich missionary, but she is ugly, wow."

Kate smiles because she was brought up to manners, VFW-Auxiliary-Style: you smile at men's jokes. She always laughed at her dad's jokes. But it is horrible how men judge women as ugly or beautiful! Who went to a caucus and sent in a resolution, reading, "I want to be ugly?" It is cruel to be judged for what you didn't vote for and can't help!

Henry James was the genius of End-Action-by-Figure-Barely-Forewarned. He would set up a whole story, with the people in it, and then—in the end—fast, theatrically—in walks one of those barely-mentioned people to make some huge difference. It is fun to write a story like that. I commend it for the fun as well as the unity.

An example of artistic introduction of character is Raymond Carver's "A Small, Good Thing," one of the greatest short stories of our time. It is a beautiful, major story about a beautiful, major subject. It has wrath in it, but all the human beings are respected and shown to have tremendous mercy-giving potential. Terrible things happen in Carver's story—one, a natural catastrophe, the death of a little boy from a head injury; another, the wrath of the baker who had contracted to bake a special, personalized cake for the boy's birthday (which never took place, the boy having died before that Monday). The baker, on whom the ingenious, heart-filled ending of the story depends, is introduced lightly, carefully in the very first scene. In that first scene, he is a disappointment to the blithe mother of the little boy.

> The baker was not jolly. There were no pleasantries between them, just the minimum exchange of words, the necessary information. He made her feel uncomfortable, and she didn't like that. . . . she gave up trying to be friends with him.[4]

Neatly done: perfect introduction of a character who for starters makes a main character "uncomfortable" and with whom "she gave up trying to be friends"—when at the end he, who owes them nothing, will be exactly the friend they need.

Why must we mention each character at least twice if not three times? In a novel, characters come and go; in a short story the mind of the reader attributes *more symbolic meaning* to the scant people and props and events. It isn't that readers are educated to do that. Uneducated readers do it, too. It is psychological fact: the shorter a pronouncement, the more each part of it means to people. Look at how people read a tiny Bible passage. "Consider the lilies how they neither toil nor spin, yet Solomon in all his glory is not arrayed as one of these." The lilies and Solomon are emblazoned with our attention. So it is, somewhat, with a short story's people.

Since every object and every person in a story have so much burr to them, we can keep a feeling of a *unified* work of art only if each character pops in a couple of times at least. No one writes a first draft, of course, with such manipulation. Only when we have decided upon the cast, do we check for double mention or appearance of each person. That way, when the reader comes across that person the second or third time, he or she feels at home in the world of this short story: the reader feels trust in the author's little world given. "O yes!" the reader thinks comfortably, "That's that character again, who *belongs* in this perfectly made little world I've escaped into." The reader is like people who belt the refrain of hymns.

Another reason for second or third mention of a character is the deepened significance of anything seen a second time, but I will discuss that in Chapter Eight with reference to *things*, rather than people.

Point of View

Finally, once the cast of characters is chosen, we have to decide on the point of view. This expression, point of view, will be used so much in this book, I will use its usual film and television abbreviation from now on: POV. POV· Natalie will mean "from Natalie's point of view." There are texts and texts on POV—one of the shortest yet most complete being a part of the introduction to *The House of Fiction*, edited by Caroline Gordon and Allen Tate.[5] Janet Burroway has a first-rate discussion of POV on pp. 223–305 in *Writing Fiction*.[6]

A good rule of thumb is to have one character's point of view and stay with it throughout a story. One rule that may *not* be broken is that if POV is inside one character—seeing things which only that character could see, you can't change to *inside* another. One may start with what is called the "Butler's Introduction" (POV the butler or POV an omniscient narrator) and then move to inside one character. A classic example is "The Dead" by James Joyce, in which story we start POV Lily, the caretaker's daughter, who "had all she could do" to keep up with taking the gentlemen's coats, sending the ladies upstairs, at the beginning of the Miss Morans' annual party. Only Lily would use the phrase she "had all she could do . . . ", but as soon as Gabriel, the protagonist of the story, comes in, the POV is Gabriel—or omniscient author hovering just above Gabriel's shoulders. In novels, the POV often shifts from chapter to chapter: chapters, in fact, are arranged so that the author can shift POV. In a short story, one POV is nearly *de rigueur*.

I do not discuss this further out of humility. I have nothing new to add to the discussion. Everyone who has a text on how to write short fiction gives attention to POV. In brief, there are two literary abilities that divide master from apprentice:

1. Ability to keep POV in control, and

2. Use of particulars instead of generalities

We will be looking at how to stop writing generalities, how to stay with the particular, the singular rather than the plural, parts rather than wholes of things, in Chapter Nine.

CHAPTER FOUR: NOTES

1. Mark Helprin, "The Schreuderspitze," *The Houghton Mifflin Anthology of Short Fiction*.

2. Anton Chekhov, "Gooseberries," *The Houghton Mifflin Anthology of Short Fiction*.

3. Mary Doyle Curran, *The Parish on the Hill*, Little, Brown, Boston, 1950.

4. Raymond Carver, "A Small, Good Thing," *The Ploughshares Reader: New Fiction for the Eighties*, ed. DeWitt Henry, Pushcart Press, Wainscott, NY, 1985, pp. 69–96.

5. Caroline Gordon and Allen Tate, *The House of Fiction: An Anthology of the Short Story with Commentary*, Scribner, New York, 1950.

6. Janet Burroway, *Writing Fiction*, Little, Brown, Boston, 1987.

Chronology in the Short Story

Leaving the First Draft:
Working for Theater and Moral Intensity

There is no issue on which writing teachers differ more
fiercely than whether or not stories should run chronologically. I belong to the conventional school: I believe that the
final version of a story will be strongest if the plot runs
chronologically. I believe a good deal of the *present time* of
the story should take place *before* any interior-monologue
backflashing is allowed.

   This theory is based on two psychological guidelines: first,
that after our first draft we must drop all self-service and begin
to serve *only* the content of the story, and second, we must
devise for our story the kind of psychological effects which
literature can have: theater and moral intensity.

   If theater and moral intensity are what we really want,
then we need to drop their opposites away from our first
draft. No matter how lovingly we wrote, we must drop toneless realism and interior-monologue backflash.

   To make the point, I will use as "the gesture of toneless
realism" the most common beginning of all children's literature and adult novels and stories: waking up, turning off the
alarm clock. There is almost no way for a character to wake
up interestingly: for every Gregor who wakes as a beetle, there
are the millions of other characters who wake and do *nothing
that is interesting for the whole first sentence.*

They wake and yawn.

They wake, yawn, and reach over to turn off the alarm clock.

They wake, yawn, turn off the alarm clock, remember that today was the day that . . .

They wake, yawn, turn off the alarm clock, remember that today was the day that . . . and put one foot on the cold floor. (Never warm: I have literally *never* read a story in which someone touched foot to a warm floor, although there are dozens of writing conferences in Southern states.)

It is natural to write toneless gesture plus interior-monologue since that is the way first drafts develop in our heads. It is the way, in fact, in which we work ourselves up to *any* further intensity. Our knowing that conversation is going to have some intensity to it before we are through doesn't keep us from our starting with small talk (toneless gesture).

Here is an example of first-draft writing: toneless gesture followed by interior-monologue backflash:

> The alarm went off. Peter waked, yawned, reached over to turn the damned thing off. Oh no, he thought, this is the day when Natalie's parents expect us at The Lake.
>
> He remembered how keen they were on showing him and Natalie their new retirement place up there—the town was St. Fursey, but their cottage was actually on George Lake. He groaned. They were so goddamned *expressive* all the time. They never learned to just be realistic and calm and human. Yes—human.

It is hard to get into a story fast, just as it is hard to initiate a conversation which will be interesting right from the first. Generally, we agree to a bland format something like this:

Small talk

Checking in about relatives—births, marriages, deaths

Praise for the surroundings if one of the speakers owns it (A property-loving touch: do proper socialists praise one another's leased farms? Probably not: they probably praise what the owner *does* own—propagated plants or flowers.)

Mild, evasive approach to the intense issue

Intense conversation *re* the intense issue

Since that is our habit in conversation, we are likely to use it for first drafts. First drafts are closer to life than art.

In real life, Peter would *not* greet his parents-in-law at George Lake with

"Hullo—hullo—good to see you, sir! You both look wonderful. This is a wonderful place, still got White Pines without blister rust—what a fine sound that soughing is! You bet I want to see around before lunch! I have always admired how you two brought up Nat with so much originality. The way you told stories at dinner and you read aloud to her and all. She's got to have about the best imagination of any woman I know—on the other hand, Jesus, people, I wish you had given her *some* sense of reality. . . . She doesn't have the least respect for how things get done in the world!"

The mother says, "You're right! She has very little respect for how things get done—chemical warfare and who knows what else!"

The dad: "Way to go, Natalie!"

Peter: "All very well for you two who live off private income! I run a research institute, and I can't lift my nose at every whiff from the lab! Or from the president! Or from the media! I need to have things go smoothly—like a wife who is sober at public occasions, for starters!"

Since we don't start off conversations so precipitously, it doesn't come naturally to us to write stories in which strong feeling or forewarning of strong feeling appears at the beginning. We know so many toneless, realistic gestures: we have to keep ourselves from falling back on them:

She twirled the swizzlestick to gain time.

He caught the waiter's eyes. "Four more all around,"
he said.

He ground out his cigarette.

She started dialing.

They squinted out over the lake.

A word on literary strictures: I am making literary strictures in this chapter—pointing out kinds of writing which
come naturally but which make second-rate literature. Before
explaining why realistic-gesture-cum-interior-monologue-
backflash is weak, I would like to discuss briefly the 1990s
dilemma of writing teachers.

The 1960s and 1970s wisdom was (rightly) that human
beings are designed to be writing creatures—and that if people
don't write with satisfaction, someone must have stunted
them, blocked them, and deprived them of enough education.
Our brains have in them the millions of neurons ready to
enjoy writing. As Yeats said,

> The good are the merry,
> Save by an evil chance

I have already described the various ways in which Jill, the
creative-writing student, was bent by bad teaching from a
good writing career (Introduction to this book).

Because we do so much encouragement of everyone to
write, there are now thousands of people writing journals and
memoirs and stories whose writing education consists almost
solely of having been "encouraged." Their teachers, they tell
us, were "open, encouraging, flexible, nonjudgmental," and so
forth. Goodness knows we need texts to cheer us on. We
need some praise for our first tries. We want the questions
asked of our first drafts to be friendly questions—not
challenges. "What else might that character do?" is a friendly
questions. "What you've got that character doing doesn't
work: whatever made you put that in?" could be called an
unfriendly question. We need first-draft encouragers who
will not ask the unfriendly question. We need first-draft

encouragers who will be like islands we lonely swimmers can wash up onto. We need a more noble voice than the commercial-handbook philosophies.

Most teachers at The Loft, the Minneapolis-based writers' organization, regard their job largely as giving encouragement. They and their students talk a good deal about teaching creative writing in a way that will be "open." That word has risen above its riverbed and widened over adjoining terrain. It has come to mean nonjudgmental and flexible (its original, psychotherapeutic meanings), tolerant to casual behavior, Democratic rather than Republican, more approving of tofu than of steak, more interested in writing journals than careful poems, indifferent to literary fine points, and culturally relativistic. The writing courses taught at The Loft and elsewhere in the United States since the early 1970s have produced a generation of people not much instructed in how to work on *second and subsequent drafts*. It is hard for them to make major structural changes in what they've done. Thousands of people now writing don't really know anything about literary structure. Some of these people believe that advice to revise for literary effect is "elitist."

Elitist is a word which emanates from our thoughtless mass of U.S.A. junk language the same way white smoke comes off dry ice. Other words like it are *hierarchical, baggage* (when used to mean memories of past injustice) and *white-Western-male-dominated*. In a University of Minnesota course called "Literature and Politics and Ethics" (1987), I referred to Lawrence Kohlberg's idea that healthy human beings are innately interested in moving from simple to complex thinking—that we all, if not blocked, will move from amoral thinking to elegant, imaginative, ethical process. Two hands shot up. One student said Kohlberg sounded like a Western male elitist: who wants to go up through any stages? The second student said she despised Kohlberg's hierarchialism. Both agreed one must crawl before walking, but suggested we stop talking about "stages" because it reinforced hierarchical thinking.

I am certainly for encouraging people to generate the first draft of their hearts' desire, but discipline's wanted for the work to follow. It is mindless pain-avoidance not to give up ease for major structural work in second drafts. A new difficulty is that most writers expect to "correct" their first draft on the processor—scrolling up and down changing small points. For structural re-envisionment, alas, we need to print out and handle the sheets of paper, looking at a spread of them. That is unaccustomed work. If we don't do it, however, we will be like someone who so much admired his or her first charcoal drawing, with its rash, handsome strokes, the artist was unwilling later to assign any values to the lines: there stood the dark strokes of full charcoal. There stood the untouched white paper.

I'd like to return now to the drawbacks of fiction that leads off with a toneless gesture followed by interior monologue:

1. The first action will be common.

2. The backflashing traps you in the POV of the character who made the toneless gesture. It is a less intense, mystical experience for a reader to be inside one person so fast than to feel—for a little longer, at least—the sense of a wise, storytelling narrator who will tell us how things happened *in chronological order*. We want the sense of the author's presence just behind the shoulder of whichever character stands on scene.

3. Interior monologue *immediately* drops pace. All that part of our mind which asks, "What happened next, Mom?" is slightly let down when the backflash comes in.

4. Since backflashing is used so much by artless writers, it is very worn, and therefore bores the reader with a stale mechanism.

In the short story, we have to work much more quickly than we talk, in leisurely conversations anyway: we have such a dense, symbolic form that it needs sharp starters. Let's look at a first-rate start-off to a great short story, Joseph Conrad's "The Secret Sharer":

> On my right hand there were lines of fishing-stakes resembling a mysterious system of half-submerged baboon fences, incomprehensible in its division of the domain of tropical fishes, and crazy of aspect as if abandoned forever by some nomad tribe of fishermen now gone to the other end of the ocean; for there was no sign of human habitation as far as the eye could reach.[1]

It is one of the most encrusted of Conrad's many encrusted sentences, but his word choices make us feel moody and brooding—ready for his psychologically strange story:

a mysterious system

half-submerged

incomprehensible

crazy of aspect

as if abandoned forever

now gone to the other end of . . .

no sign of human habitation . . .

It is no good retorting, O well—but he was just describing such scenery as needed for his plot. Or he was just describing some scene he remembered from real life, and wanted, as amateur writers say, to capture it.

Conrad was too much artist for that. First of all, it is partially true he wants those details for plot. But he could have used others which were not "mysterious" or "half-submerged." He chose *those* details because they *were* mysterious or half-submerged—which suits the spirit of his story. As for his simply choosing some scene he recalled: Conrad was an old hand. He was psychologically grown up: he would never sacrifice artifice to personal nostalgia. It is only beginners who try to serve three masters—one art, of course, but the second, to whom they have trouble giving notice, being their own lives, a third being to do a *roman à clef*. "But that's not what happened!" beginners cry. Or, "That's what she really *said!*" It is hard to leave the master called One's Own Life, and to serve the less pain-assuaging master, art.

I clearly remember being about nine years old in Duluth, taking piano lessons. I took piano lessons from various teachers, one of whom was an amateur in the sense that he didn't take music seriously and thought kids should have fun at the piano. All the other little girls got to curtsey and pull their 180° full skirts (Niagara-starched and ironed by someone) out to each side, so that they looked pretty. I wanted to look pretty, too, but my mother insisted that serious musicians do not curtsey. She showed me that drooping bow which then appalled me and ever since I've longed to do. After a reading, the marvelous poet, Denise Levertov, sometimes gives that drooping, lugubrious sort of bow—with its indifference to-wards people and its utter subservience to art.

In 1939, I wanted to look pretty. I didn't give a damn about Mozart. My mother said, "This afternoon, when you do the Mozart, you serve Mozart." Mozart the Pig, whose genius made me spiteful.

Eventually I was taken out of that piano group and given a serious musician for a teacher. He told me about phrasing. He said, "Look—let the second movement sing—let it sing!— Look!" He showed me how to make my fingers *work*—not for me, but for the music. It became clear to me that during the quarter hour I played the Sonata Facile in C, likely no one else was playing Mozart in the Northern Hemisphere—so I was minding the shop for Mozart. It deepened my current to feel that: under my Niagara-starched dress, I labored away for art, not for ego, at least for a quarter-hour. All this to say how hard to drop the self and work for art!

Mention of Mozart raises the question of people who make art as if it were second nature: they didn't need text to teach them. Here are unfair truths to recognize and then put away forever:

Not everyone needs to study in order to make art beautifully.

Some people study and never do make art.

Some people study an art and then do beautifully who hadn't done beautifully before.

Some writers do scarcely any *work*, yet they make beautiful, truthful literature.

Some writers are thoroughgoing alcoholics, and *they* make some beautiful, truthful literature.

Some writers work humbly in the service of beautiful, truthful literature and have scarcely anything to show for it.

It is neither consistent nor fair. (It never was fair.)

If we are to be angry over our work-without-much-to-show-for-it (or no audience to show for it), we should still live gently and work gently, and as Henry James adjured writers, "simply do it, do it, do it."

The Strengths of Chronological Order in Stories

If a story happens in its chronological order, the reader is free of the interior voice of any character remembering events: for the reader, this means having only his or her self, so the reader feels *there*, savoring the ambiance of whatever strange scenes are offered. C.S. Lewis was right in saying whatever else we want of fiction, we want to be taken away! away! to some strange place.

And fast.

A good example of perfect chronological story writing is Raymond Carver's "A Small, Good Thing." The first event—in the first paragraph—is the ordering of the birthday cake by the main character. It is the first thing that happens. That birthday cake ordering is the fulcrum of the whole plot. The second thing that happens is that a car hits the boy. That is what happens second and Carver tells it second. It is ten times more dramatic than if he told it first and then backflashed to the cake ordering.

By the time we've done a *full* first draft, we know what the story will be about so there is no need to weaken its chronology by starting somewhere later than its first event.

It is wise to think of the backflash as a structure weakener: you can do more of it if other elements are especially strong. If you do too much of it, you have amateurish, self-centered literature. It is like overwatering concrete: you can water it heavily, which makes it easy to mold and handle, but if you do, the mortar-to-sand ratio should be extra-strong. Or, if like the ancient Greeks you aren't using arch and keystone, you need very strong beam-strength in your stone header.

I'd like to pay close attention to how Hemingway introduces "The Short Happy Life of Francis Macomber," using a tiny backflash without destroying theater. His story starts with the hunting party having drinks, but they *all* refer to Macomber's having run from a lion earlier. Because it isn't just Macomber remembering it, we aren't stuck in the POV of just one character. Because Macomber's wife is unpleasant about it, we straightaway have insulting things said—which is always interesting. Hemingway spends a half-sentence on physical description before adding that everyone was "pretending nothing had happened," a classic attention-getter-cum-backflash opener.

A hidden use of the method is that this story is against women, not about cowardice: it is about how women are treacherous. (This is Hemingway, and that is Hemingway material.) The author, therefore, doesn't want to get into an interior-monologue sort of backflash. He needs to bring the wife on scene fast, being ugly-minded soon.

Here is how it would apply to a scene showing LaVonne waiting for Vern beside St. Fursey Lake. "Just like him," she thinks, "not to show up and here it is our anniversary and he promised he would grease the Evinrude and he isn't here."

Such an opener locks us into the mind of a small-minded person. We may have started the first draft with,

> LaVonne squinted out over the lake and thought, Just like Vern not to show, on our anniversary, too.

but in a second draft it would be better to figure out the first chronological event of that story or fragment of story, then the second, then the third, etc. The array, in proper order, gives us choice of tone:

> At breakfast LaVonne said, "Would you get home early and grease the Evinrude?" She started to say, It's our anniversary, but decided not to because part of her wanted to catch him forgetting it. "OK," he said, absentmindedly because he was already thinking of the drive south to the Twin Cities. He was going to tell his boss that he didn't like the chemical-warfare stuff they were working on in the lab.
> He drove down and told the boss, got fired.
> He drove home and other things happened on the way. He met a Unocal 76 service-station guy whose dog had been stolen.
> They got drunk together.
> Vern got home late and LaVonne was infuriated.

Once we see that list of events in order, the toneless realism of one interior voice seems a shallow way to start.

Introducing People before Weather and Props

If we discuss weather and place in the story *before* we have presented the characters, then the weather and place are only exposition, and we can't see them through the characters' eyes. On the other hand, if you bring in weather and place immediately, they *may*, provided you use laden adjectives like those at the beginning of "The Secret Sharer," add to the *tone* of the story, but they won't be a tenth so interesting as if you wait and bring either or both in later.

For example, if I write:

All afternoon the snow fell quietly onto the pyramid-shaped hills of topsoil and subsoil, and onto the folds and wrinkles of black polyethylene which yesterday's men had left on top of their equipment. Natalie picked her way along the temporary path with its signs saying "Sorry for the Inconvenience," wishing she had worn her boots after all. She could tell by the number of high-priced cars in the visitors' slots that all the engineering and management types were there. Well—so she was a little drunk because she stopped at Rudy's for one—not two, damn it, Peter, *one*—so she would be on tiptoe for his important future colleagues.

The snow grew heavier. By the time she was up the wood-covered concrete stairs, she couldn't make out the old liberal-arts-college buildings downstreet.

There is nothing particularly wrong with the passage. It loses several chances to use *exposition* as tone and as character revelation both, however. When the snow falls it is just snow: we don't see anything of meaning in it.

Say that we held up on that snow, and introduced both Natalie and some part of whatever her trouble is, and *then* brought in the snow: then we can make the snow work to mystify or magnify or make ironic Natalie's trouble:

Peter's company was taking on an elegant man, Peter's old college friend, John. Coming aboard at the same time were a dozen new engineers to work all the wonders which Peter talked about. We will have a little company celebration at four, he said, in the voice which meant, Natalie, I want you to arrive sober. "Don't I look sober?" she asked Bunt, the grad-school-humanities-student who tended bar. "Ask me any question," she told him, one hand on her hip like a chorus girl. "How will nerve gas help the United States make democracy safe for Russian children?" (Bunt grinned at her.) "Why," Natalie told him, "of course it will. They've already tried it on the rabbits and it made democracy happen to them. Do you see any lab rabbits, Bunt—even just one?—who have voted for a totalitarian government? Do I seem sober, Bunt?" The young man said, "Well, Mrs. Tenebray, you're ethical. You're ethical enough to make up for it in case they don't think you seem sober. Tell them I said."

They were already building the new institute which would have the labs. There were piles of saved topsoil and some subsoil lying around, the shape of the ancient pyramids. There was polyethylene cloth lying on top of the contractors' machinery, catching snow in its huge shiny black folds. Very mindful of the martini inside her, Natalie picked her way along the temporary path. The snow kept falling and turning the whole area into a mini-Alps—every minute it looked less like the way things were and more like the way the world looks when you are a kid— when Natalie was a kid, at least.

By the time she got past the engineers' pricey cars, it was snowing so thickly she couldn't make out the liberal-arts buildings downstreet.

It still has some Toneless Realism. Picking one's way along a path is Toneless Realism. Anyone with any sense, including a dog, would pick his or her way along any path that went through a construction area. Therefore, it doesn't tell us anything about Natalie. She is full of liquor, which in literature generally suggests that there is a *reason* for escaping into the liquor, even though in real life most drinking comes simply from habit, not immediate psychological cause.

Nonetheless, the snow has literary use past that of mere exposition: the snow hides the ugliness of the lab construction so we know—since we are inside Natalie's POV already—that she wants the ugly meaning of the lab hidden. It supports her drunken yet accurate conversation with Bunt, the bartender. The literary rule here is that we all want feeling brought in as soon as possible. Emotion-laden material is what is interesting—not impersonal exposition. The sooner we know of some devastating situation, the better. In the opening sentence of "The Short Happy Life of Francis Macomber,"

> It was now lunch time and they were all sitting under the double green fly of the dining tent pretending that nothing had happened.

not only does the author say nothing of the weather, he doesn't get round to weather for another three pages. He uses props, and props only, to give us *place*: double green fly of the dining tent and canvas cooling bags. Because the details are not American Suburban, and because we have had the line about "pretending nothing had happened," Hemingway can do a backflash soon afterward without boring us. He demonstrates other skills: people are the subjects of the main clause—not things. There is more emotional and ethical commitment in any sentence which has *people* instead of *things* as its subject—a reason, by the way, for so much bureaucratic writing and armed-forces rhetoric in which people *never* are the subjects of the sentences: no blame, no shame, no credit adheres to things as they would to people. Look:

> . . . what is central to bureaucracy is specialization and the standardization of tasks and the rational allocation or assignment of these tasks in accordance with an overall plan. Collective tasks may thus be broken down into component tasks which are means to a collective end.[2]

That is conventional social-science writing which would be livelier if people instead of the things (specialization, standardization, allocation, assignment, tasks) were the subjects of the sentences.

> Bureaucrats by custom or habit or conviction deal out specialized tasks to people: they deliberately plan that people do standardized work. It means employees must do absolutely pre-assessed kinds of work in order to accomodate a pre-configured whole.

Since the authors, Compton and Galaway, were not interested in generating any ethical *effect* at that point in their text, they lost nothing of purpose in having things, rather than people, as subjects of their two clauses. Most educated Americans read a good deal of such prose—that is, books whose authors want us to stay cool and assess the layout. Unfortunately, that kind of prose—useful in the social sciences, dead in art—is in our ears by the time we are old enough to write short stories. Our habit is hearing it. We have to make a conscious effort to break the habit, because we *do* want "ethical effect" in our readers. We must break the habit of dead-feeling prose just as consciously as a child raised among a family of thieves must (if he or she wants to live as a civilized person) deliberately break the habit of clipping people, chintzing waiters, and sharping in card games—and all the other casual ways to steal which seem sensible enough if you have been raised in a nasty family.

The idea that people must be in a natural scene to make it interesting is not new. William Blake pointed out that we people the scenery so that we can love it. Sir Walter Scott's openings are weak. There's too much nature—too much description of the lea at dusk before we are allowed a glimpse of the distant figure makings its way across the lea. I never thought that nature description of Scott's was endearing. One longs for human feeling. We want the image of ancient feet before we get too much of England's green and pleasant land.

A Listing Format

Richard Brautigan wrote a stunning short story called "The World War I Los Angeles Airplane," in which the story is simply a list of thirty-three items in a man's life.[3] The thirty-third is a repetition of an earlier item. By the time all thirty-three are stated, the reader has been given the personality of a man of generosity not taught generosity by his society. He has a sense of beauty not taught by his background. It is one of the loveliest stories I've ever read. It is three pages long.

We can learn a chronology lesson from Brautigan. It is that if a meaningful scene, no matter how short, is set next to another meaningful scene, feeling and value multiply. The reader rejoices in the queer, abortive spaces between these brief scenes. Let's try it ourselves. Let's say we half-see in our mind's eye a marvelous or horrible character. Let's pretend (not writing but simply reviewing in the mind only) that we are doing his or her autobiography. Then let's have a piece of paper with thirty lines, numbered. Then choose thirty events or half-hours in that person's life and write them down. Then think of the most telling of those scenes—and repeat it, for item number thirty-one.

Such an exercise returns writers from the jagged world of disturbed chronology.

"That Is the *First* Thing I Thought of: What Is the *Second*?"

First and last, our problem is to make literature surprising. What constitutes surprise is the same thing that constitutes humor: *more* truth and rather more *accurate* truth than one expected in the circumstances. If you read through jesters' remarks in Shakespeare or reread some of Garry Trudeau's dialogues in *Doonsbury*, what strikes as funny is the exorbitant amount of truth some people notice while others only say "Huh?"

The best way to work surprise into a cliché-ridden manuscript is to ask, as you reread a sentence, a phrase, a plot outline: "That's the *first* thing I thought of: now what is the *second*?" That procedure leads one to refine the first guess, which might have been simply a cliché of modern pop-psychology. Since psychological clichés are as prevalent as any other kind, we need ways to get rid of some of them.

First, make yourself eschew the first version of a scene, knowing your second will be more accurate. For example:

> Peter stood near the door, shaking hands with the two women and three male engineers who came in. He had memorized their names twice—once, a week ago when he first got the list and then again last night. It was too late to wait until the day itself to glance over a learned list like that: nervousness spoilt his memory. So he had done it last night and now he greeted each. He liked them anyway: he especially liked all these people because he knew their names and he knew he was a man of the world who could coordinate all their efforts in a way *they* would be glad of. He knew that engineers, of all the employees in the firm, and this Institute would be no different, tended not to "buy into" the ideals of the firm: they tended to define their job description as technical and finite, not communal.

That particular insight made him look down on engineers, but today he did not. He liked their boyish and girlish faces. They weren't subtle-looking, but they were Americans who were straightforward, who wanted to do a job. He had a glass of Perrier in his hand, pretending to drink it, but the reason he had it was that he meant to hand it to Natalie the moment she came in so it took up her hand which otherwise would so easily reach for the white wine.

Then he made out a figure he hoped to God was another woman engineer whom somehow they had forgotten to mention to him, please not be Natalie, picking her way around the new construction area, barging into a parked Audi, O God. But of course it was Natalie and he thought, in swift succession: I wonder if I could divorce her. No, I cannot. We don't abandon women in our family—especially weak ones. Why can't she be—he thought—looking at the rosy, really fairly pretty face of Angela Blackbury, the biochemist who had just taken a glass of the god-awful Chablis—why couldn't Natalie be like her? Ready to go, Ready to *live,* for Christ's sake, instead of showing up loaded all the time?

That piece of interior monologue isn't much but it has two strengths: we hear Peter *think three different feelings in succession.* Instead of saying to myself as I wrote it, have I got it right? would he really think that? I made a deliberate sequence of things he might think, one after the other. It is an easy way to write. Besides, people think chronologically in large part. They see the drunk wife, they think (1) something wrathful. Next, having thought the wrathful thing they remind themselves (2) of their abiding principles. After doing that adult, ethical thing (which an adult and consciously if not unconsciously ethical person might do), they (3) get wistful (for a happier marriage in this case).

It gave me a chance (as author) to have Peter long for a woman who seems more game for *life* than Natalie—yet have that woman who looks so vibrant to him be a chemical engineer who is designing nerve gas, now for rabbits, later for people. And the reason Natalie is drunk is—well, we don't thoroughly know that yet, because the story isn't over and I have only begun to think about her. This is only, say, the second or third draft. I never get the real tack of a character until the third or fourth draft.

We are getting Peter, though, through interior monologue. We have paid the price of interior monologue, too. That passage shows his character some, but it stalls the pace.

CHAPTER FIVE: NOTES

1. Joseph Conrad, "The Secret Sharer," *A Short Story: Thirty Masterpieces,* ed. Beverly Lawn, St. Martin's Press, New York, 1987, p. 103.

2. Beulah Compton & Burt Galoway, *Social Work Processes*, 3rd Edition, Dorsey, Homewood, IL 60430, 1984, p. 183.

3. Richard Brautigan, "The World War I Los Angeles Airplane," *Studies in the Short Story,* eds. Scott & Madden, Holt, Rinehart & Winston, 1980.

CHAPTER SIX

Dialogue

Keeping Good Tone Despite the Dialogue

Again this reminder: please do not think about any of the technical considerations of Dialogue while still doing the first or second drafts of a story. Always go at the first drafts without any literary gear. If we have launched into a dialogue in which two distasteful people are speaking distastefully to each other, in which neither is admirable nor even pitiable, our unconscious mind generally won't join the project. Disdain feeds only itself. Very likely this one psychological fact alone keeps so many writers in writers' classes stuck doing unpleasant, shallow work. If, however, we let the same two distasteful people talk to each other in a beautiful setting, then an affectionate balance is present and the unconscious will stir itself. It likes irregularities anyway. "O great!" it says. "Ugly people talking mean in a beautiful place! Perfect!" it rouses, to see what else might go into the scene.

The psychological regimen here is to remember at all times that however dreadful the characters in your story, there are some things in life *you* like. If the only life you like is camping in British Columbia, make yourself a mental image of Skihist Mountain in the early morning or the North Thompson River. If you like the ravines of the Blue Ridge Mountains, then remember them, the raw clay and bright mica of them.

In case this sounds absurd, please know it is not. It is a common Social Work practice. Say the client comes in with a broad sweep of complaints: life stinks, everything is unfair. People stink. The welfare system is corrupt. The United States has a foreign policy like ancient Rome's or worse. Most people are like Drexel underneath their smiles. The client presents, in other words, a full sack of depressing observations, very groundful, well-taken complaints, perhaps. What does the social worker do? He or she says, "Right on all counts! It is clear you have a good, strong ability to express yourself. What else is going on? Why'd you come in?"

The client had 100% disgust. Because the worker identified and praised a good thing (character quality) in the client's *own* life, the client's disgust has come down to 75% to make room for 25% satisfaction with at least that much of the self—75% vs 25% doesn't sound like much of a balance. If we lived in Nazi Germany in 1938 and were noticing the plethora of evils, we wouldn't feel much assuaged by being told that no one, but no one, grew Carpathian Harebells more beautifully than we. In other words, a balance of *feelings* does not imply a balance of the real evil seen and the real good observed: it means only that one is staying capable of the whole gamut of *feeling*. The evils are still there.

Any balance of feeling, any ability quickly to identify several different feelings coming fast, going fast, some of them noble, some inaccurate, some so self-centered it makes you sick to think over what you felt two minutes ago, some gross, some grateful—any ability to move around through a variety of feelings is enlivening. Social worker and client, for example, will return their talk to injustice or unkindness. Those are the subjects one goes to social workers about; those are the human activities social workers know how to help us with. Since the client has talked about things felt as evil but has also, because the worker told him to, talked about things he saw as not so evil, or even as good (such as Skihist Mountain or the North Thompson River or Mount Pisgah near Asheville), the client has distinguished *differing* feelings. No longer does "everything" stink. Incidentally, if there ever were two untherapeutic comments they are 1) Everything sucks and 2) Shit happens. The reason they are unhelpful, untherapeutic is that they are *general*: sanity is in distinguishing evil *from* good, not lumping opposites.

Now that the social worker has got the client breaking apart bad from good, the client is not so much a victim of disdain or fury as a sane person *studying* a bad patch. This is the best ambiance to write literature in. You can social-work yourself a little:

Client: "I seem to be writing appalling stuff about appalling people. What's the matter? Can't I be simple and love life and have attractive things to say about life?"

Social worker: "You know what's good about you that I've noticed so far? You take on the big ones. When you see what you think is horrible, you don't do a denial on it. You have some detachment. You're willing to focus on being truthful, and you don't keep an eye out for the main chance (charming the audience). All you need to worry about for now, I'd say, is being balanced and accurate. Good luck. Check in next week. Don't skip."

The discussion of dialogue which follows is designed so that the author and reader can experience a strange mix of wise listener, passionate moralist (if the dialogue *does* handle great doses of evil or good) and balanced person.

Realism: Inner Versus Other

Americans nearly all enunciate English badly. Likely only six or seven hundred Americans pronounce the word *twenty* as *twenty* and not *twunny*. Very few people pronounce the unvoiced *t* between two syllables: most people change *pretty* to *priddy*. Even women named *Patty* pronounce their own name *Paddy*.

If we believe in outer realism only, we would write dialogue by Americans like this: "The President of the Research Institute shook hands with each of the chemists and microbiologists in turn. 'We're happy to have you joining us. It's a priddy nice thing for us all around, cuz you will vastly enrich our researches. Let me know if there's anything—liddle or big—which I can help you with as you get seddled. Also my support staff sed to tell you the same. So our welcome is from all of um.' "

That passage is ridiculous with its misspellings. Literature does not imitate life exactly: literature is symbolic by definition, so mispronunciation in literature symbolizes bad breeding or ignorance. I used to be fascinated that in the 1930s or 1940s the Katzenjammer Kids said, *wuz* instead of *was* in the balloons of their cartoon. Since both words are pronounced alike, I couldn't (at age nine, ten, eleven) see the sense of misspelling the word. Of course, what the author was doing was showing them to be ignorant and provincial in every way he could. "Wuz" is to tell you that the Katzenjammer Kids did not go to St. Paul's.

Outer realism is especially weak in small tight forms like the short story. If I were presenting President George Bush in a short story, I would not have him say "didja? huh?" even if I heard him say "didja" instead of "did you" sixty times on television. *Didja* in fiction means a genial, uneducated person: I think of Bush as an Andover graduate serving or not serving the poor people—a very different thing.

The classical use of provincial and uneducated language in dialogue is to give all of it to minor characters. In the part-of-a-story about LeRoy Beske (the man whose black Labrador was stolen), the author could classically give some bad grammar and bad pronunciation to the VFW drinker who insulted environmentalists or who jeered at the Fursey Slough. "You want to save sloughs, huh? Lemme tell you sloughs you want sloughs. Know whatchu can do with yer slough, you can . . . ."

I don't think giving slack language to minor characters is a good idea. For one thing, it locks that character out of the author's purlieu of characters who—for all their sins—share in our planetary life together. It locks that character out of the numinous encircling which an author can lay out in a work of literature. Flannery O'Connor is a wonderful short-story writer, but I think she would have been even better if she had not let herself jeer, using such heavy provincialisms, at minor characters. She was accurate enough, about those dreadful people, but surface accuracy is not everything.

What's more, surface accuracy can be addictive. I was raised partly in North Carolina: I love how Southerners tell anecdotes with their sprightly frankness: "Mrs. Beasly was enraged at Mrs. Bemis, so one day she took and went right on over to the spring where Mrs. Bemis was cooling her butter, and she squatted down over the butter—well, I want you all should release me from telling how she defiled that butter. All that while Mrs. Beasly was defiling that butter (Southerners understand repetition), Mrs. Bemis was peeping from behind them Sears Roebuck lace curtains, the ones she declared her grand-aunt inherited from Belgium. Down at First Methodist she told John Henry Shattuck that Mrs. Beasly was as low as a copperhead in a wagon-wheel rut."

That kind of writing is fun. It is fun to do or try to do and it is fun to read. It is important to write very little of it.

One way to indicate someone is using poor language without using disrespect for that person is to drop in two or three ungrammatical usages and then let the rest of the dialogue be decent English:

> Vern watched LeRoy squeegee off the windshield. The man did his usual scrupulous job, not leaving scum in the inch or two below where the wiper pressed onto the glass. LeRoy looked as if he had been crying.
>
> "Bad day today," Vern said. "Sorry it's a bad day if it's a bad day, LeRoy."
>
> "Let me tell *you* what kind of day, Vern. If I ever get my hands on the guy stole my dog I'm going to blow him up so high by the time he hits the ground the eagles will have made a nest in his ass."

Not realistic—too ebullient—said with too much satisfaction. That would be the speech of someone *enjoying* laying out the revenge. Here is LeRoy more carefully:

> "Let me tell *you* how what kind of bad day! When I get my hands on whoever stole my dog."

Bad grammar, incomplete sentence. But not *lemme*—we keep *let me* pronounced all right, because we have enough provincialism already to indicate that LeRoy probably didn't spend twenty years at Princeton with Einstein. . . . Besides, we don't want LeRoy for some lightweight stock character: he's part of our fate, so to speak.

Filthy language is rather engaging when scant, boring when widely strewn or poured. I recently looked at a new book in which all the characters found nearly everybody either a fucking piece of skirt or a fucking piece of prick and so forth. In general, filth serves only to show that the author feels contempt for all the characters, or worse, the author's tastes have been debauched by the current U.S.A. market for literature. He has decided that 63% or 72% of readers prefer trash so he is providing trash. That is the Drexel Ethics. It is profitable, I expect.

Hemingway developed a good way of indicating filthy language without using it. In *For Whom the Bell Tolls*, people say "obscenity thy mother" or just "Thy mother" and all the feeling is there. That is literary. It works. It is more giving of the feeling to the reader than anything expletive, in the same way as "And this . . . and this . . . and this . . . " is sexier and joyfuller about foreplay than most explicit description of foreplay.

Another way to handle some filth is to surround it with beauty.

Inelegant: LeRoy snarled, "Listen you silly fuckhead . . . ."

Better: LeRoy explained his idea to Donny in the VFW. It was that Donny was a fuckhead.

That is not great, but the word "explained" at least brings in a tone more inner than naturalism: explanations, even such an impoverished one as LeRoy's, belong to the world of textual truth and clergy and the helping professions. We don't feel we are simply being debauched by the writer.

We notice whether or not an author has any toleration of

humankind generally by the respect shown or not shown the most minor characters. On the other hand, a spicy use of minor characters is that they can have a full run of shallow emotions, whereas the major characters cannot. Jane Austen was a genius at embroidering up a few flaky, wildly unconscious, and regressed human beings for each book—Mrs. Allen in *Northanger Abbey*, Mrs. Bennett in *Pride and Prejudice*, of course. Austen loved a fool, and always dropped at least one, fully shown, into each novel. Austen was not Tolstoy: she didn't care a sixpence whether fools had or hadn't the hand of God supporting them. She was a secular person.

An author can choose how serious an attitude she/he wants to take towards the people in the stories. If you choose to consider the soul of each person important, then it is wise to give that person some elegant language: we take their conversation, then, to be *inner*—to be the *soul* of the person talking, not just the provincial or ignorant or vulgar *outsides* of the person talking. I wrote a story once in which a mother dog was instructing puppies about how to get along with bullying human beings. She warned them that if they did not *adore* people and learn to stay with them even if the people mistreated them, they risked living out their lives in The Great Emptiness. I then put down, "The puppies did not know what The Great Emptiness was but it sounded execrable." Just as I had thought they might, the editors suggested that "execrable" was too fancy a word: a dog would never use it. (I love the idea of which English a dog would stick at.) The suggested alternative was "real bad." I thought it interesting that a dog would misuse the language, using "real" as an intensifying adverb when it isn't one. I have been trying out the cliché "bad" to see how widespread it is. I told a group recently that I felt confident—much more confident—about such and such a procedure. Several of them corrected me. "You mean, you feel good about yourself." Once clichés like "feeling good about yourself" or "feeling bad about yourself" get going, stopping their use is like commanding iron filings not to snuggle up around a magnet.

Since the puppies are *thinking* or *feeling* inwardly, not

speaking at all, we can say they felt something would be "execrable." It is a pejorative word.

It is as important in dialogue as anywhere else to avoid boring language. I suggest going a long way around clichés if necessary. I wanted "execrable" because I like puppies. My literary offering to puppies in general is to hypothesize their feelings in such and such a situation. There's little else I can do for dogs.

It is not my own idea to serve all the creatures with respectable language. I learned it from Tolstoy's passages about Levin's dog Laska, in *Anna Karenina*. I commend those passages to anyone who wants to see how *inner realism* can be—at least in serious work—much more valuable than *surface* realism.

Dialogue as Exposition

Lo, where the poor wretch comes . . .
[Polonius, *Hamlet*, Act I]

Some exposition would be better undone than done badly in dialogue. Nichols and May were a marvelous Chicago-and-New-York-comedy team who would ask the audience what they'd like for a first line (someone would shout one), and then what they'd like for a last line (someone else would be shouting something), and finally, what *style* they would like— all this to be an insty-play at most. The evening I was in the audience someone offered, "What if gravity fails?" for the first line. Someone else shouted, "Are there any towels in the men's room?" for the last line; someone else requested Ibsen for the style. Without even conferring with each other, the two comics became before our eyes two servants preparing an empty but well-appointed house for the great family to return to: "What if Miss Gravity fails?" Elaine May said, pretending to be dusting a chair. I don't recall the exact dialogue but it ran more or less: "Ah, Ingrid" (let me interrupt here to say that Nichols and May were such consummate artists that they not only did us an Ibsenlike plot, but they did it in the stilted, dys-rhythmic style common to translators of Ibsen into English): "Ah, Ingrid, have you got all the forks and cutlery gleaming for when Miss Gravity arrives in the large brougham, provided that this two-day snowstorm does not prevent the coachman, Oivind Jensen, from safely delivering her, the youngest of the four unmarried sisters?" "Ah, Lars!" (Ingrid replies) "if she does not arrive, then Master Thorkild's machinations with the city fathers will have been in vain, and the superhighway will be built right through the *fjos*, where our Hanna lives, Hanna whom all of the family, even though they are Bergen and Christiania graduates, have loved, because it was the milk from her dugs which gave the family strength at the time of Great-Grandfather's disgrace, and now—unless it can be prevented—old Hanna and her new calves will be cruelly de-stroyed, without a single church bell's tolling partly because the engineers whom Great-Grandfather cheated got revenge by burning down the Stave Church and they wrecked the church-yard where Miss Gravity's relations lie rotting under the snow—O Lars, we must have everything perfect for the family when they come! Have you checked? Are there towels in the men's room?"[1]

That's only a wild approximation of what Nichols and May gave us. They picked up on Ibsen's use of what is called in literature "the butler's introduction"—that is, exposition done by minor characters before the major personnel come on stage. Joyce uses it in "The Dead."

Beginning writers try to get too much exposition into dia-logue. It usually flattens the tone. A way you can make dialogue work for exposition without flattening tone is to flood the talk with strong feelings: so then the facts you want to drop off to the reader are no more noticeable than sparks from a roaring fire. Here is a roughshod use of dialogue-with-passion-as-exposition:

> He straightened up. He didn't exactly straighten up: he had been sitting up well enough, but he somehow looked as if he were making himself firmer, as if he were preparing to take an oath.

He said, "I have to tell you I hate it when you bring up that incident about the kittens—over and over! It wasn't one of Mother's glorious moments and I never pretended it was—but it also wasn't a big thing—and you keep harping on it, Natalie!"

"You mean it wasn't one of your *father's* glorious moments! No one's criticizing your mother, for goodness sake, Peter! It's your *father* who went smashing right into her room without knocking, shouting about Hitler's getting into power! and when he saw you and your mother crying, he went stamping off!"

Peter still saw it all in his mind's eye. His mother had looked up and cried, "O how could you? Can't you see Fluffy's dead— dead?" She had one hand curled around the dead kitten in her lap—not minding that its blood might get onto the grey woollen pleats. . . . Her other hand was around Peter himself.

His head had shot up: he had felt called to be a man like his dad. A man is someone more upset about Hitler, whoever that was, than about this dead kitten.

Now his wife narrowed her eyes at him. "That scene was a big thing in shaping your personality, buddy boy," she now said.

At least this last time, there were no guests present. The engineers' party was over. Peter and Natalie were eating at the Canton Wok. She was snarling at him with her whisky breath and he was snapping back, with his no doubt garlicky breath.

A man has to have perspective, he told himself for the three hundredth time.

Peter's annoyance at his wife's repeatedly bringing up an old scene from his background gives *us* a chance to see the scene without doing much clumsy backflashing POV Peter. It gives us a chance to see Peter as a person who resolutely clings to the idea that the wide world is the proper purview of a *man*—that women, on the other hand, are weak and see only the griefs close at hand (kittens' deaths). It is this view which makes him psychologically able to run an Institute where nerve gas will be perfected.

Dialogue can inform about the past, provided the present feeling—sadness, wrath, joy—is strong enough. "I am sick of you always bringing it up to me about how I . . . ." is stronger as a way to introduce a person's marriage-long habit of breaking toenails in bed than to say,

The alarm clock went off and Natalie reached out to turn it off. Morning. She remembered last night, when Peter, for all the times he had promised not to, took to breaking off toenails in bed again.

Much stronger is:

"Listen, Nat, knock it off, will you—here comes my new lab assistant, Vern what's-his-name. Come on, I want you to shake hands with him and act sober and then—well—get out, because we have to talk about his job. Anyway—hey! I heard you! Nth time! And I won't break my toenails in bed any bloody *more*! Can't you leave off about the toenails?"

Dialogue Has Its Own Devices

Here is a short list of some of them:

1. A character can talk one kind of thing but *act* or *be* quite another (e.g., Peter talks gentleman, patient husband, good administrator: in fact, he is a center figure in sadistic weaponry). Dickens has so many characters who weep out of pity for other human beings at the same time as they abuse those near them who can't fend for themselves that we can scarcely count them—Mrs. Pardiggle, Mrs. Jellyby, several of the schoolmasters, many more.

2. Characters can talk to each other, not listening, but only waiting until the other finishes speaking, and then continuing on their own line. It is true that likely this kind of noncommunication-in-communication-clothes makes up 85% of human conversation. In a short story, it stands not for normalcy as such but for what it really is: people listening only to themselves.

LaVonne: "I don't know if you realized I have been waiting here all day. You said you'd be home early."

Vern:	"A big thing happened, LaVonne."
LaVonne:	"That's why your arms are full of roses— the big thing that happened this day eleven years ago? — Where *is* that armful of roses, Vern? You leave it in the Chevette?"
Vern:	"No, a big thing today—down at work."
LaVonne:	"From the smell on your breath, it wasn't such a big thing it couldn't fit into a liter bottle."

3. Characters can literally not hear each other at all: they simply talk past one another.

VFW drinker:	"I am up to here with environmentalists."
LeRoy:	I could reach across the table and put those eyes and mouth and nose all in one bunch. If I weren't so sleepy I'd do it.
VFW drinker:	"Who gives a damn about sloughs any- how? In sixty-five million years, you know what there'll be around here anyhow?"
LeRoy:	"Your trouble is, you never really owned and loved a dog. That's why you're such a jerk. I could take your eyes and your nose and your mouth and I could put them in one bunch where you could see what you had better."
Vern:	"LeRoy, I get the feeling we should get out of here, friend."
LeRoy:	"Then I could go home and know that at least I didn't just sit here and let someone

steal my dog. *Someone* got a piece of my mind, anyway.''

4. Characters can skip to the next subject.

Donny: "I suppose you're still mad I told that little whore daughter of ours to get out of here."

Kate: "I was thinking about that guy LeRoy being so mad last night in the VF. About his dog gone. Donny, you remember that little kitten we had?

5. Characters can understand each other so perfectly they dovetail: that is, one asks a question; the other answers it exactly. They repeat one another's words a lot. When this happens, the people seem to us so in harmony we know they are in love. Tolstoy's scene with Kitty and Levin is the perfect example of this dovetailing. In fact, they understand one another so well, one just chalks first letters of words onto a table and the other grasps from it the whole sentence. It is the most perfect, symbolic job of passionate love through dialogue which I have ever seen (in *Anna Karenina*).

6. Characters can be together in this way: one of them does all the talking and the other only thinks, e.g., Peter could be talking aloud the whole time, about how wonderful his father was.

His father was an absolute tyrant, Natalie said to herself. But she kept her eyes on Peter and didn't interrupt. When she had just this amount to drink, which was usually at just this time of day—7 p.m.—she would recall how handsome Peter had been when she was in love with him.

"My father understood how weak my mother was," he was saying. "He let her be what she was. She was often in tears. I never saw him cross at her. He was always serene—and although he was a person of some importance, I never saw him act superior to her at all."

Natalie thought, O yes that old bastard the father. Well, Peter was sweet. He wouldn't know psychological abuse if you poked him in the eye with it—

7. One character can speak in direct dialogue and the other can reply in *indirect dialogue*. This has a peculiar effect. It is swift. The person speaking direct dialogue seems sincere, a little slow and pokey. The person using indirect dialogue seems well organized, a little brisk, a little distanced, sometimes a little catty.

Vern (eleven years ago today): "I love you, LaVonne. I guess I'm saying I want you to be my wife. It seems funny to think of living together all our lives! Where will it be? All I know is the Twin Cities and then St. Fursey Lake, of course. I haven't ever been anywhere."

LaVonne told him about the weekend her dad and mother and a boy she was pinned to went to Reno. They had not really had a very good time but she made it sound like fun.

Vern: "I'd like us to have a *good* life. You know what I mean, LaVonne?"

She told him she did. She used a very gentle voice. To herself, she knew she didn't know what he had in mind. Nothing much, she guessed, because at least when *she* said things like that, 'a good life,' she didn't too much have any definite thing in mind.

Vern: "We'll have a good life, LaVonne. I know we will."

LaVonne couldn't decide whether to tell him she had saved herself for him or not. Aloud she told him she didn't feel as if her past life counted for much. Everything that counted was up ahead for them. She could see by his facial expression that was a good thing for her to have said. She said it again, using other words, because, well, in addition to making him happy *now*, he would remember they had talked like this and then if he ever said anything about anyone in her past she could say, I thought we agreed it's our *future* together that counts.

So she said that aloud now, that part about their future being what counted.

Vern said, "Our future . . ."

Having Vern speak, having LaVonne only indirect, gives her a tricky, shabby cast. In about 90% of dialogues, one person is meant to seem shabbier than the other one. This is one of the ways in which it can be accomplished.

The Physical Building of Dialogue

We have conventions in how we talk to one another which do not translate well onto the page. One such custom is the beginning of sentences with one word, then a comma (or pause of some sort), before the content of the message starts:

How are you, LaVonne.

Oh, fine, I guess.

Well, OK

Well, all in all, OK

Oh, well, uh, yes, and *no* are the most common one-word-plus-comma responses. The two-word ones, particularly among casual linguists, are legion: *I guess, I suppose, well yes, well no, not really, hell no.*

What such usages do is provide continuity. A human voice queries; another answers. No unfriendly silence occurs. Ever since radio came to the world, silence has slunk out of fashion. Before radio, a pause suggested that someone was thinking—and thinking might be noncommunal. We know that thinking is private as nothing else is, so if one does not wish to seem separate or superior or standoffish, one fills such a silence with, "Well now!" The practice hit bottom with the Bay Area's 1960s custom of starting a sentence with "Like" plus a comma. "What is the dress you are sewing?" "Like, it has a bodice." "It has like a bodice, then it's got like a skirt, a dirndl, like."

We are left with a good deal of it. The way to handle it in fiction is to take a ruler in hand. Most American rulers are 1-inch or 1-1/2 inch in width. Lay the ruler vertically on top of a page of dialogue already written, slide it all the way to the left so its left edge lines up on the left margin of your print. Then draw a vertical line down its right edge. That cuts out all of the one-word-plus-comma openers. If you then remove those so cut, you have clean dialogue. If the sentences of the dialogue opened with the addressee's name-plus-comma, still take it out. It will make the content of the dialogue leap forth: it will remove the mass-culture-sound of extra low-key, unfelt words.

> "Duane, I want to talk to Mr. Tenebray if I can."
> "Well, lots of people want to talk to Mr. Tenebray."
> "Well, this is different."
> Duane never liked Vern Schwach. (We need a last name for Vern. "Schwach" = weak in German.) He didn't even like the man when he had on his lab coat and was working. When the fellow was knitting his eyebrows over his nose and looking cowardly, Duane liked him less. He itched to push his face in, kids' playground fashion. Humiliating him in conversation would do as well now.
> "Look, you want to tell me what it's about or do you want to get out of here, because I'm busy."
> "Well, I guess that's not much of a choice."
> "No, it isn't. What's it going to be, Schwach?" As Duane heard his own voice, he knew he meant to fire this man. He hoped all the eyebrow knitting was about something big enough so he had an excuse to fire him without clearing it with Personnel.

A ruler laid down at the left side of that exchange takes out these words: *Duane, Well, Well, Look, Well, No*. It leaves a bare, but just as realistic, exchange:

> "I want to talk to Mr. Tenebray if I can."
> "Lots of people want, etc."
> "This is different."

Deliberately dropping one-word-plus-comma openers seems artificial if you are not sure what the dialogue is to be and are sketching it in for the first time. Don't torment yourself by cleaning up dialogue on a first draft. Once you have made a mental image of the scenario—a mouse of a fellow named Vern Schwach bravely standing up to some nasty intermediary between the lab staff and the gentlemanlike Peter Tenebray—then you are glad to have a way to pick up the pace: the fewer the words, the starker the feeling.

Sometimes a suggested "rule" of writing feels inimical. To check whether it actually is useful or is only a half-cocked notion of some textbook poseur, have a look at the dialogues of authors you like. If you look at Tolstoy, Hemingway, Mansfield, Austen, or Helprin, you see how very seldom any begins a conversation with one-or-two-words-plus-pause. (I am assuming that the translators of Tolstoy tried for rhythms comparable—low-key and a little slack—to the original Russian.)

Nearly everyone lays out dialogue in just one cadence. We have to make a deliberate effort to vary cadence. Alas, the problem with habitual writers of journals and diaries, who do not take tough classes with serious teachers, is that no one makes them stop and hear the length and sameness and slackness of their sentences. Alas, there is a dreamy, wise-eyed sort of contemplative roll to long sentences. It is the devil of dull prose. One of the first things good composition teachers show students is how to insert a brief sentence with some slap to it after two or three longish ones.

There are some nice ways to alter dialogue rhythms. In the examples below, a long wavy line indicates the actual speech which a character has made. A short wavy line is simply some shorter speech.

First most common, tiresome rhythm:

"_____," he said.
"_____," she said.
"_____," he said.
"_____," she said.

That is how children will write dialogue if you leave them to it. It is businesslike enough: it gets everything said which he and she want to say, but the rhythm is tiresome.

Second commonest, tiresome rhythm:

"_____," he said, "_____."

To break up the dull rhythms shown, first, vary the length of the lines spoken by one or the other character. Second, transpose the "he said" with the second part of anything he said—if it helps the sense of dialogue:

"_____," he said.
"_____," she said.
"_____," he said.
"_____," she said.

Below is a replacement of the he-said and she-said part with a second piece of conversation by the same character:

"_____," he said.
"_____," she said.
"_____," he said. He said, "_____."

It is pleasant and a little surprising to see the two "he saids" together like that. What's more, it lends an odd significance to the second part of his speech.

A third way to make dialogue fresh (although it won't break up dull rhythms) is to change "she said" once in a while to "she told him."

Good literature uses very few other words for "said." "She went on" is all right if it is used sparingly. "She repeated" is weaker than saying "she said" plus the repetition, because it has a thread of Author Intrusion.

Some words for "said" are used *only* by terrible writers. They are "mused," "smiled," "maintained," "adjured," "reminded," "gasped." These are bad-fiction-glitz and on their own can wreck a passage of literature.

If you use adverbs with "said" or "asked", you are making a choice: does the adverb tell us the *character's* POV of how she or he spoke, or does it tell us the *author's* POV of how the character spoke? It is more elegant literature not to use adverbs *unless they are POV the character*:

"Did you hear the one about the boa constrictor and the Missouri Synod pastor?" he asked wittily.

That example uses the adverb "wittily" POV the character: presumably the author doesn't find the remark witty. When the author says "wittily," in fact, it reflects on the character's judgment of what's a witty remark and what is more likely a patched-up cut at the Missouri Synod Lutheran Church.

When the adverb doesn't seem appropriate to the context of the speech, then it is the character's POV; the author looms ironically behind, letting the character have that opinion.

> She spoke in her usual genial tone, modulating her voice as she almost always did. "You are such a goddamned phony, Peter," she said. She had had plenty to drink. She felt pretty cheerful. She had on her Alistair Cooke accent, modulated, kind, unmistakably philosophical and classy. She said in a gentle, modulated voice, "You suck, Peter, honestly you do."

The POV is somewhere behind Natalie, close to me, the author. There are three people making up the gist of that passage: one is Peter, the gentleman with a defense contract; the second is Natalie, an alcoholic whom Peter (enabler that he is!) will not take into treatment since *her* dependency, despite its bad breaks of moral attacks on him, *works* for him—he is good, she is bad) and finally I, the author, who am terrified of people who consign eighteen- to twenty-five-year-old young men to five or six hours of agony followed by their death.

An Argument Against Starting Stories with Dialogue

Dialogue is a poor way to start a story, although some great stories do start with talk. It sets a gossipy tone which in turn delays your being able to set a tone of any consequence. Playwrights are stuck (or blessed) with dialogue right from the first: in the case of short stories, it is useful to ask, do I really want to start with someone speaking, which means we have a human voice as the first element? Or do I want a line of ambiance?

Say someone said, "Will, of course we like the play, but could you do us a short-story version that we can have as a reading on audio?"

"Right," he said:

It was well on into Advent; the stars moved in their own slow, icy streams. Rime lay thin all over the hipping and castellations.

Finally the new man came on. "Has that ghost shown?"

"Not a sign, thank God, not yet. There aren't supposed to be ghosts this gracious time of year"—and so on.

I think the first sentence helps with ambiance. But I have another reason for liking a sentence of description or action before a character speaks: it is that commercially trained writers are told "you must catch the reader's interest immediately! Dialogue will 'intrigue' the reader!" and other advisories which make my lip curl. To "intrigue" the reader, thousands of hacks begin:

> "Just try that once more—just once!" asserted the red-faced man, as he lifted his stein and made to threaten LeRoy with it. The man exclaimed, "I will lay you out flat as a penny on a railroad track!"
>
> "Yeah? That right?" cried the angry LeRoy. "Well try *this*, you dog thief!"
>
> "Hey!" ejaculated Vern to his friend LeRoy, two friends who had been together that afternoon and now were involved in a brawl at the VFW Post of St. Fursey, Minnesota. "That guy isn't the man who took your Labrador, LeRoy!"
>
> "He looks the type of guy would, though!" the man LeRoy expostulated.

There's a tricky I-know-how-to-*manage-the-audience* tone about starting off with dialogue, not to mention the amateurish, awful ways of avoiding "he said." We don't feel that the story is a cordial gift from the inward part of the author to the rest of the author, and secondly, a gift of both inward and other parts of author, to the reader. It lacks respect.

It is a sort of junk-bonding between writer and audience.

CHAPTER SIX: NOTES

1. Nichols & May. Mike Nichols and Elaine May, a comedy team who started in Chicago, performed in New York, and made very funny records.

How Stories Take Place in a Place

The Attractions of Having No Physical Setting

Moralists and young writers have this in common: craving to tell stories which have no specific sense of place. They want the story to be set "just anywhere" because it could have happened to everyman or everywoman, anywhere. They want the story universal; we readers can supply our own mental image of some place which seems relevant to us.

Such stories are infused with mood. I love to read them, about once a year, no more. I love these parables without specific place in the same way that Unitarians love occasionally to attend a fundamentalist or at least very orthodox church: they get to belt out the old hymns about blood and eventide. Their hearts fill with simple gratitudes. Yet they know, and of course this is why they don't regularly attend these fundamentalist or orthodox churches, that they must return to more difficult, less oversimplified ideas soon.

Stories without place are invariably barnacled over with morality. That is lovable, too. After all, our 1990s world is a world of sleaze. It is peopled by sixty-year-olds who suppose that most twenty-eight-year-olds are materialistic: it is peopled by twenty-eight-year-olds who can't fathom why so many sixty-year-olds will not give up their huge portfolios full of defense-industry dividends. In the CBS *Nature* series, we learned that large cats are not *perfect* mothers: if there is a severe scarcity of game by February or March, the large mothers will take the game and not share with their young who are too small to claw for it. When I first saw that, I thought: oh, then, they are just as horrible as *we* are—big people stealing the world's wealth from small people.

Given that kind of morally-anxious backdrop, the parable is rather refreshing once in a while.

There is a spiritual health about no-place-setting for young writers. People's brains long to crystallize ideas. The brain likes to put a hold on any occasion it thinks it recalls from somewhere else, and then scan back over its miscellany of memories to find the somewhere else and arrange it together with the new story, thus making a new category. Let us say you lived a life of forest—only forest. Then one day a Northwest Airlines plane went over and you noticed it (of course). Years went by. One day a pilgrim came through with a red rucksack. Your mind would scurry back, scanning, scanning, until it put that rucksack together with the rudder and stabilizer paint of the Northwest plane. "Red," the brain growled with satisfaction. "I will make a new category and it shall be called *red*."

A common age for making hundreds of categories is eleven or twelve. (Who sticks with concrete thinking if they can invent theory?) It is the age for breaking away from incessant, merciless reality. Millions of eleven-year-olds lay out whole private continents or islands now sunk in the sea which used to be there; these young writers draw maps of them. They name some of the people and animals. Those secret lands are the homes of our crystallized ideas. If they don't grow up to read a lot of literature, they will always have it in the backs of their minds to do a story about utopia. Dozens of utopian science fictions in the 1950s alone were written under pseudonyms by M.I.T. professors: those men (they were males, as it happened) were living out the old dream which had probably lain about in their heads since they were eleven.

If that dream doesn't get lived out in childhood or in secondary-level or college-level or in science-fiction level stories, writers will want to live it out whenever they get to it. We are an animal that should mosey about in abstraction. It is a natural and I think, numinous, stage. Like any developmental stage, wanting to write up plots which have force-of-soul but no setting is universal (we all go through it or could, if not blocked). It somewhat responds (like all stage development) to friendly or unfriendly environment: if a child lives in a gritty family of (1) no humor and (2) no abstract language at dinner, that child may take cover in fantasy as long as possible. Some children are so psychologically deprived, they can't even organize their minds enough even to *get into* fantasies of their own making. These children are later vulnerable to charismatic leaders who promise them "their ancient glorious past" (fantasy) or who offer them scapegoats (fantasy). Children brought up in 100% practical families where all the conversation is daily occurrences, technical breakthroughs (from the Dad-in-the-garage-workbench level right up to space aircraft) are likely to keep their eleven-year-old utopian writing very much to themselves. No one wants to hear any patronizing, affectionate jeering. Their minds, never hearing the abstract language of ethics or aesthetics, will—if they burgeon into abstract thinking much at all—most likely vector into engineering or scientific thinking. They come to moral ideas very late. Some of the weaponry experts who have "turned around" about military values got to that stage only in their early or middle old age. The practical, technical childhood background stalled them—a kind of moral vacuum.

The Psychological Uses of Utopian Writing

In our stony American life, both parents are away so much children have little hour-for-hour time with their Significant Adults. Peers don't help one grow up much, if at all. College-entrance studies suggest that the eldest of most sets of siblings have the best chance of getting into a first-rate college: the reason appears to be that the eldest spend early-years time with adults, whereas the younger children spend more time with each other.

Here is a logic to consider seriously: If writing about utopian, moralistic, or at least ideal lands is a natural stage of human ethical growth, then we should provide a VERY friendly environment for it.

Otherwise we might bump further along towards a vicious society without turning this twentieth-century insight to use. The short story author Frank O'Connor believed that a measure of a nation's ability to act civilized is how much serious fiction it produces. Germany was his case. (Since music has no ethical component, it isn't germane to the discussion. People were slow to welcome Walter Gieseking to a post-World War II American concert tour because he had played to the Nazis all through the war. But if he had been a poet or story writer and had given *readings* to the Nazis, we *never* would have asked him.) Stories like Theodore Storm's *Immensee* do not wake the moral spirit: they are perfect escape, so they don't qualify as a civilizing influence. O'Connor did not know the work of Marie Luise Kaschnitz, or Christa Wolf.[1] Germany no longer makes the perfect or only Horrible Example, but what if O'Connor was right?

What if there is a social-psychology connection between amount of fiction read and viciousness of culture? Since 1945 American magazines have nearly all dropped the three or four fictions in each issue, in favor of "practical" features. That means, the child raised in the gritty practical family has one less access to the fantasy he or she needs. What if this is serious? It sounds neurotic: it also sounds neurotic to worry about the electromagnetism generated in transformer canisters which stand, two to an alley, in most American cities, causing, it seems, two to three times the incidence of leukemia in children in houses near them.[2]

We need idealized *story*, as such, for at least the following six reasons:

1. It gives experience of other than oneself.

2. Story presents the ideal case.

3. Story teaches us to recognize and despise evil. Despising evil is an acquired taste.

4. A story writer, while you're reading his or her work, is treating you with playfulness and courtesy.

5. Stories get you blessedly away from your peers for a time, and

6. Stories identify your own fine feelings which you may otherwise have not noticed.[3]

If all of the above, civilized goals are furthered by attention to story, we should regard the utopian, unplaced or pretend-placed works of twelve-year-olds and of beginning writers as a psychological *good*.

Like other psychological landmarks, idealized story wants honoring. Next, we should leave it behind. I suggest that if you, as writer, crave doing a placeless story set in simply all time or any time, with an *everyman* or *everywoman* in it, that you write it with dispatch. Give it a whole weekend. When you've finished it, make it beautiful. Sell it if you can. Then save it for family, friends, and yourself. Bind your own copy (not the magazine copy, if you sold it to a magazine) beautifully in an Acco-press binder with William Morris print papers glued on. Then keep it forever. It is one of the various reserves of your soul, like cold water kept cleanly in mountains high above the city.

Next, give up the placeless story in favor of great complexity. It was a form of spiritual health to write a utopian story or a cleanly, slightly archaic parable, but it isn't a good habit. Here is why: characters having feelings *in a place* are more vivid to the reader than the same characters having the same feelings *without place*.

Examples:

Feeling without a setting

He could see she was bracing herself in her own cold column of feelings. "You deliberately—deliberately!—got laid off?" she finally said. She said then, "No—not laid off! That happens whether people want it or not. No, not you, Vern! You deliberately got yourself *fired*!"

Feeling in a setting

He could see she was bracing herself in her own cold column of feelings. Behind her head, behind her trim body, lay St. Fursey

Lake with its evening shine, its few millions of tiny bubbles living their one split-second of life on the surface. At the far end of the lake were all the waterskiers wading around their boats, the playthings of ordinary people: "You deliberately—deliberately!" she was saying—"Deliberately got yourself *fired?*"

The second version gives the writer a chance to try a symbol or two. If the symbols look corny, out they can go in some subsequent draft. There's time. In this draft, the symbols are the millions of short-lived bubbles, of whom Vern and LaVonne are two. And LaVonne's athletic trim is the other symbol: it's her body, not her spirit, which she keeps in good condition.

Physical Setting for Contrast

If you look through short stories you are fond of, you notice that very good writers put high-toned conversations into muddy places (Chekhov in "Gooseberries") and low-toned conversations in serious, dignified places (Tolstoy in "The Death of Ivan Ilyich" has Peter Ivanovich trying to get a fourth for poker at Ivan Ilyich's wake). Good writers try to use the *lesser-known parts* of good places. Maugham continually takes care to show us *back entrances* of places. He makes himself notice whether or not the bamboo shades are dusty, whether the six-weeks-old *Times* lies on a rattan or a teakwood table, and how if one looks out over the lagoon you also see an edge of the kampong where women hold babies sired by British civil servants.

In real life, the lovers go to Deauville or the southern shore of the Mediterranean or to Lake Tahoe. They look out over the beautiful water, which we've all been told 3,200 times is a symbol of motherly feelings. They say words of love to each other. So we have it in our journals. Last time we went to a good waterside we wrote, "This is gorgeous. Use it for backdrop for a love scene." Our next step is to say: "This is gorgeous. Use it not for a love scene, but for some unusual scene, something totally surprising." Remember Camus so wonderfully describing the happy midnight swim of two men who find they can be profound, good friends to each other— *in the midst of a plague*! That is the best use of a midnight swim in the Mediterranean that I have seen.

It is useful to fill one's journal with ugly behavior or sad events which can later be set into a beautiful place. When I was a young mother without running water or a washing machine or dryer, I used to drive, late at night, from our farm to the little town where the laundromat was. All we poor people used the laundromat at night, when the husbands could care for the children at home. After I had my clothes in two or three machines, I got up high onto a corner of the folding table. I sat there, exhausted, peaceful, very proud of myself for being a mother not only by day but by night. Sometimes the owner of the laundromat came over, with his mop in hand, and told me about the effective little drugstore blackmarket he ran during World War II on a southern shore of the Mediterranean. He had been one of the paratroopers dropped into the Mediterranean in the USAAF snafu. He swam to shore and started a small, courageous extra-legal business. It was a let-up from the constant dose of military life. He felt the army owed him: the logic was mysterious and to my mind, absolutely justified. If he had drowned with the hundreds of others, would the Army have admitted to his parents that they killed him through drunkenness? No. He was right: the Army owed him. I thought, some day I will set a quiet, moon-drifted sea, a famous place of history, behind some stalwart small-time crooked operation. I will put a small-engines shop in front of a beautiful Minnesota Forest where some of the White Pines have not yet got Blister Rust.

Making Your Own Fresh Assessment of Places: Eschewing Collective Opinion

After you have broken the habit of putting beautiful events in beautiful places and ugly events in ugly places, the next practice is to reverse your first opinion of a place. At least, don't believe other people's assessments of a place unless you absolutely feel the same way.

Sometimes the truth is the opposite of statements generally made—on any subject. Here is an idea I learned wholesale from the poet Robert Bly:[4] when some notion is bruited around and around, and sounds like an authoritative refrain in your ears, try saying aloud the exact opposite of it. That is sometimes the truth (for you, at least this time around).

Here is Katherine Ann Porter in "Holiday," talking about steep roofs.

> The narrow windows and steeply sloping roof oppressed me; I wished to turn away and go back.[5]

As soon as I read that remark, I thought, what an original, refreshing writer Katherine Ann Porter was, and how wrong she is about steep roofs! Right then, reading that remark in 1985, I recalled how much I loved the steep roofs of west Duluth in the 1930s. The West End was then not a classy part of town: its boxy houses, some of whose owners kept up with painting while a good many others didn't, ran up the escarpment of Lake Superior. Along the ridge near the top lay the Skyline Drive, on which my parents took us children for Sunday. How like medieval towns, really, this west end of Duluth was! Those roofs really looked like roofs on Christmas cards.

"Mother," I said, from the back seat of the Packard, "Those houses look like the houses in a fairy tale like that— the way they go up the hill and have those steep roofs."

She said, "Darling! Daddy has driven us all the way to the Skyline Drive so we can see the beautiful harbor and the marvelous Aerial Bridge! Lots of cities have nothing like this—nothing! Don't waste this chance to see what is beautiful!"

She was a writer. She liked beauty. I was going to be a writer, too—and I like the weird feeling I got when I found that what was assumed to be ugly (the homes of the poor) was in fact classical. The fact that it got me a scolding about taste made me know the more firmly that it was a *truth*. The secret of literature, which conventional people don't guess, is that writers are forever looking for the *surprising revelation*—not for reinforcement of collective wisdom.

Periphery of Place:
We May Be Neglecting It in Order to Avoid Pain

Arnold Bennett's introduction to *The Old Wives' Tale* is a gorgeous example of pulling in periphery (placing the Five Towns—Britain's industrial pottery area around Stoke-on-Trent—in the universe). I first loved his novel's opening for its grandeur of setting. I thought, if I ever write anything, I will have the grand view like that! People are timid, however. I didn't give the grand scape to any story until I was fifty-nine years old; even then it wasn't so much a universal setting as a time-remaining-in-the-universe setting. I will discuss *future* and its relationship to *place* soon.

Noting the periphery of a place gives the story characters dignity as members of a wider community, which counts for something. When LaVonne was infuriated by Vern, because Vern turned whistle-blower about the nerve-gas lab and, like most whistle-blowers, got fired, LaVonne was standing on the shore of St. Fursey Lake. Vern could see the houses of workpeople on the far shore. Vern's ethical problems are his own, but the workmen on the far shore of St. Fursey were fired by a plywood factory because they made a union stand for higher wages. The plywood factory reorganized itself under another name and, at least in theory, with another Board of Directors (the kind of thing Dickens had the knack of so well in *Bleak House*); the factory next hired plywood workers—but not any of those who had been union-members. The union members went broke: they fished. They put out snares in winter. In summer they hung around doing ratty projects to make money: they farmed various breeds of domestic animals (yes—*domestic*—cats, dogs, rabbits) for their skins, just like Cruella de Ville in *101 Dalmatians*.

Those men and women and their spouses are part of the moral periphery of St. Fursey. I love Jane Austen. I reread her six novels about every ten years, but she is ethically a Two or Three on a scale of One to Thirteen. Except for honoring honest farmworkers, Mr. Knightly honoring Robert Martin in *Emma*, or Edward disliking "ruins" in *Sense and Sensibility*, for example, Austen lived isolated from the fate of people different from herself. She knew one class and decided to write about what she knew. Morally speaking, her opposite is Virginia Woolf who deliberately, when thinking of Arnold Bennett, thought also of a poor working woman (Mrs. Brown in "Mr. Bennett and Mrs. Brown") and whose *The Three Guineas* takes into account a tremendous number of kinds of suffering brought about by how groups of human beings make subsets out of other human beings.

We can thank Virginia Woolf for forcing writers never to allow themselves the illusion that all human society is not connected. Of course, the idea of all of human society being interdependent is dear to biologists, feminists, social workers, and physicists, and it has always been upheld by the best of the serious writers, but it is not always dear to literary critics.

Nor, to the best of my knowledge, are short-story writers regularly taught to ask, as they lay out the later drafts of their story,

Where are the *others* who live around the edges of this?

What is the landscape around the edges of your protagonists' properties?

Who or which animals are in the *other* laboratories and offices?

Every field of work, even literature, offers its own reasons for letting its practitioners be self-centered. It is cozy to be self-centered—comparatively painless. Pain avoidance is a *major* human psychological activity. Here's a rough working list of normal psychological activities:

Wanting love

Wanting power

Wanting fullness of life for the very fullness of it—travel, weird adventures, close scrapes, madman and madwoman insights; and then, without exception,

Pain avoidance

Since English Departments tend to be run by their elder members, British taste rather than ethical anxiety wafts about through the creative-writing coursework. Besides, liberal-arts educated people do not read much in the social sciences: they have a stake in regarding social conditions as *eternal verities*. Having a taste for eternal verities makes one as unlikely to be thinking up ways to make the poor less poor as Homer would have been to think up ways to get a seamen's union going against slave-driving maniacs like Odysseus.

English teachers over fifty, what's more, have been warned all their adult lives that "Author Intrusion" and "Propaganda" spoil literature. The true case, however, is not a choice of Author Intrusion and Propaganda on the one hand, and symbolic-in-its-fabric literature on the other. The hammer of literature is not the hammer of the propagandist: all we writers of fiction have to do is place victims and heroes in a scene vivid enough so that the reader makes a mental image of 1) our main characters and 2) the victims of our system or of bad luck. Providing mental images is essentially a literary tool.

To ethicists, even situational ethicists, using mental images for perspective is such a central and simple notion that we might ask why older English writing teachers so rarely advocate getting the sociological periphery into short stories. Here is a short list of some reasons I've thought of: there may well be others more to the point.

1. University creative-writing teachers of "advanced" classes notice that their students are really not advanced at all: they are not ready for fine points like sociological periphery and ethical setting.

2. People over fifty who teach English now were not told, at Andover, or Cheltenham, or Mora (Minnesota) High School, or Putney, or Upper Canada College that "one aim for you young writers, by the way, is to change the self-satisfied unconsciousness of privileged First World people."

3. People over fifty who teach English stalwartly chose a field which they knew would not make millionaires of them: they sometimes forget that they chose it for pleasure (all the wonderful reading you get to do—and the summers off); they watch their friends in private-sector business get rich as the decades go by, and they regard themselves as unmaterialistic idealists—people who do without a good deal of luxury some other people get their fingers on. Well, they growl, they have a right to "psychic income" in return, haven't they? Economists say people who don't get "real" income want "psychic income." It is psychic income to be able to live cheerfully inside your hobby. If the world has to be changed—all that painful political and sociological stuff with the awful language usage of the social-science people who ply those kinds of trades—it is "psychic income" to feel that that's their purview, not ours. It is no accident that English Department members who take the trouble to train themselves in psychology, counseling, or social work, receive overt contumely from their conventional colleagues.

4. Reading literature and being an expert on it is a nice hideaway for people who dislike challenges. Like Bartleby, thousands of people no doubt would "prefer not to." If you are one of those thousands, yet have to make a living, you look around for a quiet, untroublesome career; there is no rule that says all human beings must get their teeth broken at a Republican campaign carpark in Chicago or near Seabrook, New Hampshire, and their bodies killed at Kent State University.

5. Finally, there are corrupt people in this field as in any other. If a writer wants money, the commercial-minded writers' magazines, of course, remind him or her that what makes money in our debauched society is *escape reading*. Escape reading should be sexual, if society is sex-minded. It should be violent if society is murderous by habit. Above all, it should help the reader *avoid* moral pain. Corruption of any one kind seeps into neighboring territory, of course: if you have a corrupt auto industry—say a company making a car which needs oil changes periodically when it could be making a car which doesn't—the used-car dealers will get corrupted; they will assure their customers that if a car doesn't need oil, there's big trouble. Soon you have corrupt service-station dealers who sell unnecessary oil.

The same is true with literature. If there are coteries of hack writers appealing to the base or lazy instincts of a riffraff readership, soon there are bookstores purveying more and more pain-avoiding literature. Soon there are English teachers as an inadvertent type of used-literature dealers, assuring their customers that this is the product—this is the reality—status quo—violence, vulgarity, and recreational sex.

That is my current five-part explanation for so many American short stories having impoverished sense of *place*.

The Sense of History and of Future in a Place

What about sense of the *past* in a place? Straight off one wants to shout, "O for goodness sake! Can't we just put in the surrounding area—or the past of a place, such as in this town where there used to be U.S.A. forest and Indians and all, just because it's *interesting*? Can't literature just be *interesting*? Does everything have to be prickly with values?"

In serious literature, a passage can be interesting for its own sake with this proviso: that nothing terrifying to do with evil or good is being swabbed off in order to keep the surface "interesting." If we were writing a short story set in Danzig on September 30, 1939, it would be silly literature if there were no reference, however remote, to the fact that Nazi Germany appropriated that city the day before. Basic morality of the liberal-arts sort requires that such a monstrous activity get at least some mention.

When the political situation is not monstrous, great writers write their fiction peacefully enough—the good ones putting in the *banlieue* for the cultural interest of it. We don't always read Aldous Huxley for the argument: sometimes it is delight enough to see the building and hear the voices.

Some moral perspective is intriguing on its own: there is the beautiful first paragraph of Tolstoy's *Resurrection*. Neither Bennett nor Tolstoy would have sketched in their geographies so peacefully if they had lived in the age of acid-rain and Chernobyl fallout.

I feel especially certain of it in Tolstoy's case, since, in describing how spring came, he swings a full-force haymaker on greedy adults who instead of enjoying the weather God gave us are concentrating, as always, on figuring out ways to cheat one another. They pollute the sky with naphtha. They pave over the rich earth with concrete. Tolstoy was the kind of captain who takes the conn when we are steaming into evil waters. He would not have ducked mentioning our nuclear fears nor our dismay at cruelty and lying.

Using the *past of a place* is such a lovely literary offering, I am not going to discuss it except to remind writers to use it more. Honeywell, a gigantic and impressive tooling manufacturer, decided not, after all, to use sacred land of American Indians as a testing ground for Honeywell large artillery. If one were writing a short story and knew about that struggle between Native Americans and Honeywell, one could write a little about Native-American use of the land before the weapons range was ever contemplated. The juxtaposition alone is interesting. In ethics, we ask, who are the invisible people affected? It's a good question for writers.

Sometimes we present the past as a *contrast* to an immoral or insensitive or monstrous present. (Honeywell now,

Native Americans earlier). Sometimes we present the past as a metaphor for or *parallel* to the immoral or insensitive or monstrous present. The best such case I know of is Tobias Wolff's "In the Garden of the North American Martyrs." In this story, members of an upstate New York English department are pretending to interview a slack-hearted, slack-minded English professor from the West. In fact, the department has already chosen someone for the job. They are interviewing this poor woman only to fill their affirmative-action process. The cruelty within the department—on the part of someone the interviewer had *thought* of as an old friend doing a favor, on the part of the tiny-minded, microscopically small-minded men—is impressive all by itself. A *tour de force* from the author: the wretched protagonist had noticed that the Iroquois, very cruel people, committed terrible atrocities. They got away with inhumane practices whenever they felt like it because they had power. This English teacher went on and on, giving a wild speech about the Iroquois, telling how they cut strips of flesh from the living body of a Jesuit priest named Bebeuf, yet the priest kept preaching to them until they cut out his heart . . .

At that point, the chairman of the English department in question jumped to his feet. There was a pause. Then the job applicant used the last minutes before they would throw her out:

> "Mind your lives," she said, "You have deceived yourselves in the pride of your hearts, and the strength of your arms. Though you soar aloft like the eagle, though your nest is set among the stars, thence I will bring you down, says the Lord. Turn from power to love. Be kind. Do justice. Walk humbly."
> Louise was waving her arms. "Mary" she shouted.
> But Mary had more to say, much more; she waved back at Louise, then turned off her hearing aid so that she would not be distracted again.[6]

The first three-quarters of the story lives on its gossipy particulars: like J.F. Powers, with his Roman Catholic priests and the housekeepers and converts and parishioners around them, Tobias Wolff knows his theoretically high-minded profession, English professors and instructors. He knows all about behaviors shabbier and motivations shallower than those the profession would boast of. As I read along happily like someone listening to really foul gossip, watching Wolff's characters bristle and lie and prevaricate and abrade each other, I thought that my feeling at the end of the story would be respect for the author's ability to present grunge with humor. I hadn't any expectation of what a *turn* Wolff would swing into at the end. I rejoiced that the victimized Mary tripped up the unscrupulous Louise, by connecting with a tortured priest from *the past* of the same place where she herself suffered.

A brief word about putting the *future* into short fiction: until the 1980s, the future has been the stamping grounds of science fiction as a matter of course. Science-fiction writers except for Orwell, Forster and Huxley have been prognosticators of what effect on the earth present behaviors would have. Science-fiction writers did and do it awfully well. They generally fore-imagine outcomes along the lines of totalitarian bureaucracies, and how that part of Earth now called the United States turns into a kind of chilled magma after the big meltdown. I don't see any better *ethical* use of the future than science fiction makes.

However, in the 1980s we received a sixth and seventh psychological disappointment: our sure knowledge that humans can spoil the earth's surface and air; and finding that our universe, and others trillions of times larger of which ours is part, is flying away from its central point of creation. We supposed we'd always been here, but Stephen Hawking tells us our universe began four billion years ago. Knowing a definite starting time wouldn't be unnerving unless we had some idea of having been around forever. The trouble is, Hawking tells us there is a four-billion-year cutoff at the end, too. As Hawking himself points out, timelessness is more comforting to an egotistic frame of mind than delimitation. For example, people feeling threatened are prone to snarling, "Yeah, well that's how it *is* and it's always *been* and it always *will* be!" Einstein himself so disliked what his own formulae told him about the universe that he deliberately hypothesized and for a while, clung to a concept he called "anti-matter," just to make his answers less sad. At last, he admitted to himself it wouldn't do: all systems say the world is flying away from itself at gigantic speeds, and our earth, the livable span of our earth at least, is good for another four billion years.

Four billion years is so long we feel it as a very slight ripple in our consciousness. Yet if it is any part of our consciousness, it participates inside us as emotional experience, like a sparrow's fall. It is in there, along with pleasure and renewal in love; joy in the dark rocks off Kristiansand; fear of losing one's muscles, teeth, and hair; love of heavy air in the fore-and-aft mainsail; and gratitude for birdsong. Since it is in there, it is a business of literature to recall it for us.

Let us look at three other disappointments in human consciousness so we can get a grasp on the stupid *lag* between scientific discoveries and writers' use of new truths.

1. The world turns out not to be terracentric after all: the then-universe (which is all, so far as people knew in Copernicus's time) was solar-centric.

2. Human beings turn out not to be a creation apart after all: they are animals, like lions, apes, mongeese, and ticks. If they are sons and daughters of God, then these other siblings—lions, apes, mongeese, and ticks, are also sons and daughters of God. It makes God seem much less scrutable or much less benign.

3. Human beings turn out to be neurotic after all. They have monstrous ways of behaving. They have little control over their unconsciouses. They love to herd around in groups, but when they do it, their behavior is generally even *more* monstrous.

The Nazis showed us all that conditioned followers and technically superb bureaucrats will obey orders to murder.

To the above disappointments then, we add this: all we ever felt to be firm and eternal is relative to the speed of light. This particular finding, not so palpable as the others, nonetheless is real because it rattles our *terra firma,* our firm ideas, our firm stands on things. Things used to stay things; wave lengths stayed wave lengths.

Lest this seem an affected or extravagant argument, let me run up this old flag of stale normal psychology: one way human beings stay sane is by compartmentalizing. When you compartmentalize, you needn't keep scanning, scanning, scanning: you needn't keep checking for signals of danger or love or main chance. You can just check for *one* kind of signal in any one compartment. On the highway, we scan for danger. At the workplace, we scan for main chance. In our houses, we scan only for love.

When women surged into jobs in the 1970s, they discovered the ease of compartmentalization. I say ease, because in the home they had had to scan for love *and* danger (to children). Men who have not been househusbands or caretakers of children have no idea of how exhausting and slightly crazying it is to scan *both* for love and danger. How easy, women discovered, it is to go to work at a workplace! For another six or seven hours one need not be a responsible mother! All one has to do is practice a workable balance of avarice and ethical scruple. When the day is over, we shove briefcase back into the Chevette. On the highway, we get to stop scanning for main chance: we need worry only about danger. Soon I will be home! I remember rejoicing to myself in my car. I will not have to figure everybody. I will not have to read between anyone's lines: I can just love those creatures, who are my children, and hang out around the house and yard with them, provided all is safe. They and I have no power agenda, no hate agenda, no fear agenda. Such compartmentalization of experience is like changing games. We *were* playing cops and robbers, but we got tired of it. Now let's play house.

The mind loves to arrange the units by likenesses and unlikenesses. It is great fun. But it gives us what social workers would call "an investment" in those units. We have done intellectual work to get the materials and hours of our lives organized. We don't want these neat, discrete units to flow back into the chaos before creation, when light and dark were not separate. (The most satisfying passages in *Genesis* are those about God dividing inchoate material from other inchoate material, then getting Adam to name the animals. Everything is supposed to *stay stuck* so we can relax in it.)

If everything is relative to the speed of light, it hasn't stayed stuck. I have to add this new little annoyance (it is about 2% of my total list of anxieties) and the next time I write a short story, if I am to write truthfully I need to think of myself as the author who is—say 40% anxious for peace and ecological outcomes, 40% anxious for financial security, 15% anxious about a joyful social life, 3% anxious for Miscellaneous (one needs to leave some Anxiety Options open, of course), and 2% anxious about my universe being ad hoc when I thought it was forever.

In family therapy, when one member of a rigid, dysfunctional family grouping suddenly perceives tougher truths than before, all the others shift their perceptions. They now must relate to one another slightly differently. It is the same with feelings. If there are new ones, we need to regroup to get them all placed.

How shall we get unease about the planet into short stories? I have tried this only once so far. Cheryl's fourteen-year-old son Freddy was being bullied on the schoolbus. Mom paid little attention to his mention of it each afternoon when he got home. Like most people, she figured he was mostly "just talking" since much of *her* talking was just talking. It never crossed her mind that she could do anything for Freddy. Here is Cheryls' thinking: "Freddy'd better take it up with his dad. I'll tell him that. I mean, like there's always been some bully on a schoolbus, and there's always some fourteen-year-old boy who hasn't got his height yet, so someone leans on him. Goll, even she and her friends bullied an ugly girl in junior-high school. They flattered her by asking her to their slumber party. Then they told the ugly girl they were going to make her beautiful. They gave her a permanent like you've never seen! Cheryl just had to laugh—remembering it! They crimped that girl's hair so bad she didn't dare go to school for days. Goll, what a ball!" But Cheryl hid her smile and listened to young Freddy telling her about the schoolbus.

Everything is static: Freddy gets bullied. Cheryl giggles

over junior-high-school memories. Nothing different is going to happen. All the author has done so far is

1. Feel nervous because the planet is dying now and will be nothing but a cinder later, and

2. Tell about a mother whose child is suffering.

What change might anxiety about the *universe* make in Cheryl with her flaccid attitudes? Does awareness of sad ends make bland people live more vitally? Or does it make them still slacker, shallower, and more cynical? Might not Cheryl say, "What good can anyone do?"

Let's assume Cheryl might not get much out of Stephen Hawking, but she had seen a lighted globe showing the world 65,000,000 years from now. There is such a lighted globe in the underground part of Tucson's Arizona-Sonora Desert Museum. Might she be moved by it and decide to rethink her son's situation? She would figure, "Well, I might as well try *something*." Her son might as well enjoy his remaining eighty years instead of waiting until he is seventeen when he is tall enough to get even with the bully and enjoy the only seventy-seven years remaining.

So she thinks up a plan to defeat the schoolbus bully . . .

Although they beg to be scorned, this sequential thinking and plan for story work in a rough way. The good of the Cheryl and Freddy plot is the implication that everyone can care about the large things (loss of our world); even the Cheryls can act with resolve.

If worry over the *future* of our place is part of our psychic life, we ought to work it into fiction. If we don't, then our literature isn't telling our whole truth.

CHAPTER SEVEN: NOTES

1. Marie Luise Kaschnitz, *Circe's Mountain,* translated by Lisel Mueller, Milkweed Editions, Minneapolis, 1990. Christa Wolf, *Accident/A Day's News.*

2. Paul Brodeur, *The Annals of Radiation*, three essays in *The New Yorker*, June 1989.

3. Carol Bly, *Six Reasons for Story*, Creative Education, Inc., Mankato, MN, 1985.

4. Robert Bly, in an adult-community-education course, "Freud and Jung in Madison, Minnesota," 1975.

5. Katherine Anne Porter, "Holiday," *The Houghton-Mifflin Anthology of Short Fiction.*

6. Tobias Wolff, *In the Garden of the North American Martyrs: A Collection of Short Stories by Tobias Wolff.* Ecco Press, New York, 1981.

Props Large and Small

Props and Tone

All properties (objects in the story) give tone. *Place*, which we
have already discussed, is the largest property of all, especially
if it includes the stars and anything beyond them. Tone is set
in the first paragraph of a story. It is not a literary rule; it is a
psychological rule: here is an example of tone as psychology.
You have a blind date at fourteen; all of you sit in the car, the
two in front keeping their eyes and hands off each other out
of consideration for you and Chuck in the back, who have just
been introduced, and the car roves through the main street,
thence to the gravel pit where the real date will begin, going
on under the same night sky which your parents are sitting under, back of the stoop. "New moon tonight," says the boy
driving. You are pleased and a little curl of confidence gets
into your brain. "My mom's sitting out on the stoop tonight,"
you say, "to look at the stars and the moon." Then Chuck, the
student of carburation whom the front-seat couple fixed you
up with tonight, says, "Let me tell *you*, there's better things to
do in the moonlight than sit on the stoop!" Well—there went
that evening. One more blind date with an LJPFHT (low-level-
jeering-passing-for-humor-type!). Besides which, all evening at
the kegger, you will stay out of reach lest he make a submoon-
light pass . . . "O look, Chuck—there's —there's still *another*
agate!" with a vivacious cry, leaping out of his arms to four

feet away, to the 6,000,000th stone in that gravel pit which is the Plaza Tea Room of St. Fursey, Minnesota.

Tone is partly contrived: if we want good tone, we deliberately put in beautiful props early in the story. If we want sick tone or sludge tone, we get that into the first paragraph. If we are Socrates at heart, we likely won't choose sludge tone; if we want sludge, we likely can't keep ourselves from hostile tone.

Here are two examples of opposite tone set simply by choice of properties in the beginnings of their stories:

1. Robert Coover, in "The Magic Poker":

> I wander the island, inventing it. I make a sun for it, and trees—pines and birch and dogwood and firs—and cause the water to lap the pebbles of its abandoned shores . . . [then follow four clauses of description of a disused resort] . . . all gutted and window-busted and autographed and shat upon.[1]

That is the opening of a short story from a book of stories called *Pricksongs & Descants* (1969). It has its tone. The author gave us

things ruined

things shat upon

He chose and achieved the tone he intended.

2. Raymond Carver, in "A Small, Good Thing":

> Saturday afternoon she drove to the bakery in the shopping center. After looking through a loose-leaf binder with photographs of cakes taped onto the pages, she ordered chocolate, the child's favorite. The cake she chose was decorated with a space ship and a launching pad under a sprinkling of white stars, and a planet made of red frosting at the other end.[2]

If we have a look at the *nouns* in Carver's paragraph:

bakery

loose-leaf binder

photographs

cakes

pages

chocolate

favorite (by implication)

space ship

launching pad

sprinkling of white stars

planet made of red frosting at the other end

We see some of the words are specific details about a bakery (the loose-leaf binder of samples). Some of the nouns are in the wide universe of big, pleasure-giving ideas:

stars

planet

There are some fine points here, too—of the kind sometimes done by an author consciously and sometimes given to the author by an unconscious more sensitive to feeling than our ego-muscley minds:

planet *made of red frosting at the other end*

faintly says RED—a warning—and "at the other end" faintly suggests that we are going to see opposite ends of a continuum of experience, or we will see opposite experiences. In any case, what is suggested is *range*. The story is going to be little in its meaning. Yet we have two minutes ago read the title: this is what good literature can do, then: give us a story about a small, good thing in which the beauty of stars somehow will figure, in which dangers will figure, in which our planet will figure. Nor will it be Victorian drivel about stars: launchpads and spaceships are not the props of simps.

Donald Hall has told students for years that the unconscious is sometimes more intelligent than the conscious mind.[3] Poets wander into more sudden metaphor than they could consciously devise. The same is true in story writing. We won't know if Ray Carver deliberately went back through his later drafts of "A Small, Good Thing" and put in the stars in a sprinkling.

A reminder at this point: none of the considerations of this chapter should be thought of while anyone is still writing out the first or second full-length draft of a story. Remember the Hampl enjoinder: do as much generation of literature as long as you can before letting yourself start the organization (or refinement) part of writing.

Props and Clichés

The second immeasurably large prop of literature is the weather. It is the easiest prop to put into a story: all our lives, even the dullest people of our acquaintance—our parents, if they were dull; our grandparents, if they were dull; our peers, teachers, electric repairpeople, if they were dull—have proclaimed some truth about the weather. We know from summer-camp horror stories that it is scary to have a story start "on a dark and stormy night." No self-respecting kid of ten would say,

> It was bright noontime and twelve pirates sat in a circle around their captain. "Tell us a story, skipper," they said.

Our job as writers is never to use any cliché we have ever heard. Clichés give confidence to conversationalists who have low self-images. They are of NO use for anyone in literature. In fact, clichés are so deadly we give them to minor characters as symbols of stupidity. Irma Rombauer in *The Joy of Cooking* wrote that when you buy herbs, if the little jar or tin makes you wonderfully nostalgic for great dinners you've had in the past, it means they're not fresh enough.[4] They should seem rank and a little unpleasant, like a shock. It is the same with metaphor in poetry and with natural description in fiction. Our job is to present, if we can, the pirates at noon. If it is hard to make them scary in the old *Sturm und Dunkelheit* way then we must think of something new—for example,

> It was a bright noontime and twelve pirates sat in a circle around their captain. It had been five hours since any of them had used his long razor: although their skins were still white and clear, you could see the dark beginnings of the pitchblack hairs, thousands of them, getting near the translucent surface.

Clumsy, but enthusiastic—at least, that passage is clear of ever having become a Girl Scout Camp Cliché. *NO* good scoutleader talks about millions of black hairs struggling to the surface of *anything*.

A good check on weather clichés is to make sure you never put together two adjectives which people expect to find together:

bright __ __ __ __ __ day

lake so smooth scarcely a __ __ __ __ __ __ showed

sky was cold and __ __ __ __ __

sunlight __ __ __ __ __ __ __ __ into the spacious windows

and so on. All of us can pass the workbook test above. The cure is simply to ask oneself the following questions in order:

1. I said "bright sunny day": do I really want either of those words there? If I want one of them, what shall I replace the other with?

2. If I want both of them for purposes of plot, can I move them into a predicate adjectival structure instead of stacking them?

Stacking means putting adjectives together with commas in front or just after their noun:

the handsome young man—cliché. Yet if the story requires he be both young and handsome, fast (that is, we haven't story-space to *show* him young and handsome but must *tell* the reader he is), we will get away with this cliché better if we throw the adjectives into the predicate:

He was young and handsome.

Note the number of times Hemingway puts the obvious into the predicate, deliberately giving it a whole sentence to itself: he was right. It works.

Bad   The handsome young man spoke to the pretty twenty-year-old girl.

Better   The man was young and handsome. There was a twenty-year-old girl standing right at the edge of the gravel pit. He went over and spoke to her.

It takes space, but it avoids oily surface. There is a log of dignity of tone in the predicate adjective use. I commend it.

Poor   The heavy, sixty-year-old man had a blue, looseleaf notebook.

Better   (break in rhythm, too): The man was sixty-five-years old and heavy. He was holding a notebook. It was blue, of the looseleaf page kind.

Better to err in being ponderous than in slicking along.

Small Props

Besides setting tone, small props do a gigantic mission in artistry: almost on their own, they move a short story from exposition to memory to symbol. For this reason, it is wonderfully useful to make a list of all the *things* in your draft, regardless of how early, how late, or how slightly they appear. Next decide which four or five of them interest you most. Plan to use each of these *three times* in a story. It means looking over the whole manuscript to see how to sprinkle the three appearances back through it—making each first mention as early as possible.

A psychological fact about reading literature is this: the first time we see an object in a story, it is part of our "suspension of disbelief." We take it in as exposition. It is one of the facts we want to know about these characters' lives. The second time we see it, it is like a refrain to us: it has familiarity and we think, "That's right! This is the story which has that sort of stuff in it!" And if we are compulsively given to reading critically, we will murmur, "Good author! Got a sense of unity, I see! Isn't just following some autobiographical plan—he or she has an inward plan of some kind. . . . This is a thought-through piece of art!"

The third time we see the object, our minds attach meaning or values to it. That sounds odd until you recall how children brought up on church-hymn singing attach significance to old hymn tunes. They may grow up to become George Orwell or Denise Levertov or Rachel Carson or Michael Harrington or John Rawls, but at their funerals, they want rocks cleft for their safe hiding, floods safely sailed or skirted, ships brought safely into quiet harbors at the last—the reason: they have heard those nouns so many times the brain has processed them over and over and put them into the category stamped Mysterious and Meaningful. We do the same, on a short-term basis, in the reading of a wrought story.

Maugham has one of the most carefully built, most savage stories of our time. It is called "Before the Party."[5] It is about an appalling English family (ideal Maugham grist, of course)—the conventional lawyer-father, the stuffy and petty-minded mother with a whimpering sort of affection for her two horrific daughters—one a clubwoman whose only passion in life is being in good form and not being put in a bad spot. The other is recently back from Malaya as a widow, with her little girl. She is dour, even inimical, and the others only forgive her her unfriendly behavior, on the basis of her grief over her husband's death. The family is getting ready to go to a vicarage fête—a kind of occasion which Maugham and Queen Victoria and George Orwell all knew will be taking place untouched when all the rest of the world has cooled to a cinder. In the first page, Maugham mentions a *parang* hanging on the wall, which the widow's dead husband had brought them from the East. That is appearance number 1 for the *parang*. Malayan weaponry reappears throughout the story: we understand that weapons designed to kill people, not animals, are in the purlieu of this story. Trust Maugham.

It turns out (and this is the final appearance of the *parang*) in a hard-wrought conversation before the family goes off to the vicarage, that the daughter murdered her drunkard-husband with a *parang*. The other sister feels this is in very poor taste, and the lawyer-father feels his murderer-daughter has put him in a very bad spot. It was inconsiderate of her.

Maugham, being an old hand at stories about people with horrible values, has George bring round the car and off they go to make their appearance at the vicarage.

That's the plot, in miniature. That is the *first element* of this story. (Every story which is serious has its first, conscious element—and then some other element is brought to bear.) In this story, no one has the least real sympathy for human beings or animals. How will Maugham show that? Of course, he will let us hear the coldhearted mother, other daughter, and father speak to the widowed daughter throughout. But Maugham is a both serious and cagey writer: he drops into the story *very early* a hat with white feathers on it, which the dead son-in-law had given the girls' mother. The mother, deliberating on whether to wear the hat, since the feathers are white and theoretically the whole family is in mourning (black), decides she will. That is the number one act, which we see: she does not mourn the dead well enough to give up short-term vanity. Then she does something else: she says to herself that it is a shame to murder birds for their feathers, but how undeniably sweet of Harold to think to send them to her. Here we have more bad character:

1. She condones a violence she herself knows is cruel, by hiding behind

2. Family loyalty (gratitude to Harold for his "thoughtful-ness.")

How many Nazi killers on trial explained that they were good family men? People who are well-adjusted to doing cruel things or sleeping with people who do cruel things generally have some good family-loyalty reasons for doing them. The coarsest of them is, "Well, hell, I got a wife and kids, haven't I?" Maugham gives us his version.

These feathers of an absent, small victim who couldn't fight back show up early in the story to hint to us that cruelty will take place in this story: those with power will give a passing thought to justice, as did the mother, but not a second thought.

The bird feathers appear several times in "Before the Party." This three-time use of props is a sign of an old pro:

1. For exposition

2. To glow in the reader's memory and assure the reader of planned verisimilitude

3. The reader will feel it as a symbol of much else which is moral

Props as the Fascinating Gear of Others

We are all like small girls and boys admiring adults' tools: the more exotic the tools, the more interesting. Someone's parachute hitting against the backs of his or her calves is a thousand times more interesting than a hammer, but a hammer can be interesting, too. A cheering reminder: whatever the work which you know how to do, it is infinitely more interesting to others than beginning writers suppose. If you know how to take down a sapling poplar, cut it in half, and then lash the slighter (formerly upper) half perpendicular to the lower, stronger half (having nicked off the little branches and nubs), and then take a 5-foot-by-4-foot piece of No. 3.5mm polyethylene plastic and fasten its 4-foot edge to the horizontal slighter stem-span, and then make plastic grommet holes in the hanging two lower corners of the plastic sheet, and finally prop up the upright tree section with your toes and hands, against the fore-transom of a canoe, having tied the plastic-sheet corners to the canoe's gunwales, so that your stern paddler can use her paddle just as a side-rudder like the Vikings who never did get the hang of stern-ruddering, so you get a free ride downlake provided you've got a following wind—those details are moderately interesting to a reader, even if you take them as trivial.

When a character's equipage is not particularly dramatic, the trick is to go into more specific detail in order to attach interest. If you say that Wallich in Mark Helprin's great story "The Schreuderspitze" "got on a train to go to the mountains" to do mountain climbing, it is not so interesting as to notice that the train "pulled out of the vault of lacy iron-work and late afternoon shadow. . . . " There is another gift in this passage: we have all noted with pleasure the lacy iron-work of traditional railway stations. We want the lacy iron-work in our literature—we don't want it left unmentioned! Now Helprin has done it, and none of us needs to repeat it. Helprin has saved the "lacy iron-work" for posterity.

Helprin's protagonist, Wallich, did savage exercises in order to gain physical strength. Helprin tells us exactly what exercises were: push-ups, pull-ups, toe-touches, leg-raises. He tells us how many he did and at what time intervals he increased the numbers.

There are so few aspects of writing that are easy! Describing everyday equipment and everyday work is one, but you have to make an act of will to enjoy it. Don't ever show an early-stage manuscript (if you can avoid it) to neighbors, relations, or clergy: their unconscious agenda too often is to dampen your enjoyment tools. Think of the millions of men who served in the world's various navies during the period 1941 to 1945: how many of them noted with Herman Wouk's precision and affection the particulars of an ensign's job, a quartermaster's job, a ship-captain's job. When I worked on the manuscripts of 760 older Minnesotans, I saw dozens of memoirs of World War II service. None of them had the brilliance of detail which Wouk gleaned for *The Caine Mutiny:* when I wrote to each of these men, however, and asked for more detail about their writing, they were delighted, and they responded with marvelous paragraphs. The question is, why didn't they think to write all that detail in the first place? A question much like why is it that most people who "want to write" don't write detail of everyday life?

The conventional answer is that it takes talent to understand that detail is what literature is made of. I think it's mistaken. A less pleasant but more telling answer is that most human beings are discouraged by those nearest them from being storytellers. It isn't a conspiracy, but it is a habit. The next telling fact is that most human beings spend most of their formative years in the presence of relations, neighbors, and (except in recent years) clergy. So apparently these relations and neighbors are saying something to us which negatively reinforces our detail-recounting muscle.

Richard Wilbur has a poem on the subject of everyday joy: "Love Calls Us to the Things of This World."[6] In this joyous poem, clothes hanging on the line are angels being blown with such "halcyon feeling" that even though these clothes are just clothes for the mixed bag of humanity—thieves, lovers, nuns—he wishes a blessing on these thieves, lovers, and nuns. This particular poem is one of the loveliest short works of any time in our language: it is a poem that transforms anything you took for just a piece of reality into a piece of incarnate godliness—a perfect task for a poem.

Let's pretend we are a Dick Wilbur for a moment. We sit at breakfast in our major-sized city—one big enough to have clotheslines strung across from building to building with pulleys (as the clothesline in Wilbur's poem was). "Look, Dad. Look, Mrs. Gimball (from 2A below). Look, Rabbi. Look, Father. The clothes on that line look kind of like angels dressed in sheets, blouses, and smocks!"

As you hear in your mind's ear these people's responses, make this firm decision: whenever I feel intrigued with the beauty of any kind of props, or conventions for any kind of life, I won't check it out with relations, neighbors, or clergy.

Equipment is not quite so interesting as Hemingway thought it was, however. I distrust male absorption in technicalities when it serves as a substitute for intimacy between people. Work descriptions fail us when they are a frightened stand-in for other life. When workplace props are just workplace props, as in the marvelous work of Norman Maclean and John McPhee, then they are more interesting than given credit for. Dropcords are orange and blue—at least in the United States; tractors are bright red (International) and bright green (Deere); road equipment is heavy yellow with black trim (Deere): such colors are wonderful and should be noticed. Men and women could well spend their ninety-five years working with dun-colored equipment, but they don't, except for equipment designed for killing people (khaki, gray, or cami).

Romance publishing houses are now trying to figure how they could rope in the husbands of all those women addicted to romances. All they'd have to do is put in fifty pages broken into at least ten scenes of five pages each in which the *workplace* or ordinary people—blue-collar and lower-level management people—are described with telling details. The most engaging aspect of James Joyce's fine story "Counterparts" is not the *meaning* of it: it is the simple story of a bully.[7] What makes that story fascinating is its office details. We learn, among other things, the nightmare of making a Chinese copy. A "Chinese" copy is a legal term for a document copied so exactly that its original errors are maintained.

When we think of kit-for-life as properties in a drama, of course, any technical description is much helped if it is crowded with human intensity about some issue or other. In "The Schreuderspitze," poor Wallich is terrified by the idea of mountain climbing: he is doing it only to force himself through the ordeal so he can balance his horrible personal pain with a brave accomplishment. It is mildly interesting to hear about mountaineering equipment anytime, but it is *fascinating* to hear about it when we know the man intending to use it is terrified.

All a writer has to do to get such surge of interest into a manuscript is mine from his or her journal or diary or autobiography a description of work or equipment; look over the story plot, find a place where there is strong feeling; and plunk an otherwise low-key technical description into a scene of strong feeling. It will take the ennui out of interior monologue, in case you have too much interior monologue.

Let us say someone's old mother is to show up late in the story. She has been mentioned at least once before (to keep "unity" in the story, obeying the old law of introducing all short-fiction characters early) but this is her first actual appearance. What is her kit? Let us say she is crazy about . . . what might she be crazy about? We can give her some enthusiasms of our own, if nothing better offers: I like Fair Isle knitting. All right, let her like Fair Isle knitting. She is doing socks, at the moment. She did the feet on a knitting machine, and now will work heels and toes by hand—of a second color so they look more Christmaslike. Then she will work design into the shanks.

> Mrs. Schwach was an old raiser-of-children, from a time when helping them make snow houses counted; she had never kept up with the news. She had flunked *My Weekly Reader* quizzes when they had it in school on Wednesdays. She didn't care what man was elected to what office: she wasn't a man and didn't want to be head of an army. She wanted to make things out of 4-ounce 4-ply. She liked sailing. She wanted to have children and knit their mittens and teach them to sail. Sneer all you like: that's what she wanted, and it is what she did.
>
> She therefore brought along her knitting: its tote bag stood on the Nu-St. Fursey Motel carpeting. She was so unsure of her welcome that she had been in the motel for two hours and still had not got up her nerve to call Vern and LaVonne. It was stupid of her to try to surprise them on the day after their anniversary. Especially since it was a Saturday and Vern would be home. In fact, what if they were both—what if they were both still in bed? Yes, that's right! Now she'd thought it, she'd thought it and the idea didn't go away again: they might spend the morning and early afternoon in bed and they wouldn't be glad she called.
>
> Maybe they wouldn't be glad she'd come at all! Maybe the

whole trip was pointless. Well, not quite. Whoever owned that dog would be glad anyhow.

(She had found a hurt black Labrador on the road. It had taken all her strength to get it, but she'd done it. She got it into her back seat and she left it with the St. Fursey veterinarian. That was something. It had a collar so the vet said he'd call the owner.)

Mrs. Schwach spread out the new Fair Isle sweater on the motel bed. It was the most beautiful and complex design she had ever made. She was proud she had made it for LaVonne. She disliked LaVonne and always had. She was very pleased she had willed herself to make a sweater for her. She knew perfectly well it wouldn't give LaVonne much pleasure, but it would please Vern. Any man is relieved when his mother is civil to his wife.

She sat in the motel room, which was pretty pleasant actually. She took out her current project and started purling back, then she got to the edge, turned, purled two, and then decreased and knit away the rest of the row. I swear to God I'll call them in a quarter hour, she told herself. Or twenty minutes, because twenty minutes would bring it right to the hour. But no longer.

She half-started planning the conversation they could have. She would tell them about picking up the big dog, for one thing. Vern had always loved animals. He'd always had rabbits around when he was little.

That passage does some literary work: it shows us Vern's feelings for rabbits before his laboratory experience with rabbits. Still, it has any number of weaknesses in it: for one thing, it is all interior monologue, that droopiest of literary devices. The language is dull. It leans too heavily on the woman's being unsure of her welcome. It will need some surprise, fairly quickly, in whatever prose follows, or it will sound like 1980s sociology.

Solving the plot is not under discussion here, but crowding some feeling *from* the plot around some technical description is the point. It is interesting that African bearers (in Hemingway's day) got one pound each as tip for bringing in a lion—but it is twice as interesting because the information about correct tipping came out while we were interested in Macomber's cowardice or noncowardice.

A last word on properties as kit: there are certain kinds of lifestyle which elude the modern short-story writer. Most of us writers don't know exactly how such weaponry as nerve-gas is made or tested. Most of us don't know the very rich, either: we don't intuitively *know* whether or not we are standing in a room with someone who invents nerve gas or with someone like Peter Tenebray, who does the administration end of it.

Literature always suffers from information lag about technologies: it was thirty-odd years later before we found out that ordinary American soldiers were used as guinea pigs in radioactivity. We have to use psychological intuition, then, instead of workplace props, in our efforts to describe some of the people who make modern life what it is.

We are not always, however, going to be short of specific information about such activities. Until the Vietnam War, writers did not describe squandered bodies and the smashed brain-jell of American youth: there have always been writers who despised war and despised the middle-aged men who enjoyed planning wars—Siegfried Sassoon, A.E. Housman, Erich Remarque, Paul Fussell—but there wasn't a Tim O'Brien who showed us how beautiful a man looked as he stepped out of the shade into the sunlight, just before he tripped a claymore wire which threw his body into a tree, where it hung in wet strips. Men were sent up the tree to scrape the slick of that nineteen-year-old body down off the tree.

Once truths about evil start appearing very specifically in literature, more people will talk about them, and those who have been lying about them will start wondering if perhaps they mightn't or shouldn't stop lying now. The fact that I do not have my hands on procedures in a nerve-gas lab does not mean that some day, some writer won't report to us step by step how a nice Andover and Yale Old Boy like Peter Tenebray could do what he does. Some writer will get into the lab to see how it's done, and write up the specifics. Then people now working in such projects will blow more whistles.

As Virginia Woolf said in *The Three Guineas*, we make our moral judgments from what we know and feel. What we know and feel is enough for a start. So if we don't know the kit of chemical labs, we do know about knitting. We also can report how it cuts the pleasure of purling back a row of Fair

Isle if you imagine chemical weapons. It's our writerly job to imagine such evil because we know it is there. It is a gladder job to imagine the wonders of normal life as well. Since people love doing much of the work they do, it is our writerly job to remind them of what Richard Wilbur called "the world's hunks and colors."[8]

CHAPTER EIGHT: NOTES

1. Robert Coover, "The Magic Poker," *Major American Short Stories*, ed. A. Walton Litz, Oxford University Press, 1980, p. 744.

2. Raymond Carver, "A Small, Good Thing," *The Ploughshares Reader: New Fiction for the Eighties*, ed. DeWitt Henry, Pushcart Press, Wainscott, New York, 1985, p. 69.

3. Donald Hall, poet, critic, essayist, editor, and for many years professor at the University of Michigan.

4. Irma Rombauer and Marion Rombauer Becker, *The Joy of Cooking*, Bobbs-Merrill, New York, 1931.

5. Somerset Maugham, "Before the Party," *East and West: Complete Short Stories of Somerset Maugham*, Doubleday Press, Garden City, New York, 1952.

6. Richard Wilbur, "Love Calls Us to the Things of This World," *New and Collected Poems*, Harvest/Harcourt Brace Jovanovich, New York, 1989, pp. 233–4.

7. James Joyce, "Counterparts," *Dubliners*.

8. Wilbur, p. 233.

Small Cures

This is a short chapter on good writing in general versus bad writing in general. Its ideas are either taken from so many others that I can't mention them all, or they are my own sievings from the chaff and dust of advice which settles around writers, whether one wants them or not. The advisories in this chapter might save you time.

The following four works are the best I know of for short-story writers:

George Orwell, ''Politics and the English Language'' (an essay)

Carolyn G. Heilbrun, *Writing a Woman's Life*

Ann Charters, *The Story and its Writers*

Janet Burroway, *Writing Fiction*

I think it is a good idea to learn one hundred small rules or cures to do with writing. If that sounds rigid, just think of all the self-serving, sloppy literature the human race has produced in its centuries: think of some of the gassy writers you had to wade through if you majored in English. Wouldn't it have been a good thing if they had been forced to speak accurately and briefly, to *show and not tell* (that old saw that people can't repeat too often)? And think how the hundreds of family histories would be sharpened up if the writer went through (very bravely, of course) taking out all the Author

Intrusion—or for starters, any sentences ending with an exclamation mark.

Not to know techniques consigns you to passive experience in any field. C.S. Lewis wrote that people who fancied themselves interested in God often told him they just *felt* God. They didn't need to learn about God. Lewis's response was, Right: it's like loving the sea. You can love it without learning to swim or to use a sextant and compass or fathoming—but all you can then do is *look at it*. If you really like the sea, you will at least want to get out of sight of land. That takes navigation.

Here are a few ancient necessities of literature and some ideas on how to meet them.

Surprise

If something is expected, write something less common instead. There was once a cartoon in *The New Yorker* in which two unshaven cowboys herded some longhorns. They are very grotty-looking cowboys—not young, not from a dude ranch, not beautiful to look at. They are talking to each other. I sometimes give this drawing (without its caption) to writing students and ask them to make up dialogue for the cowboys.

"Won't be long 'til we're home, Jim," said the one.

"Hot shower'll sure feel good," replied Frank D.

That is *the first thing* the students thought of—they thought to themselves: grungy cowboys? OK—grungy, realistic, everyday conversation of cowboys.

But here is the caption of the cartoon: "Then remove the beef from the marinade and sauté with finely minced shallots and a sprig of fresh thyme."

Surprise is everything. Here is one way to get surprise into fiction. After you've written something tell yourself, "That's the *first* thing you thought of. Now what's the *second*?" You can do this check on any aspect of fiction. You can do it about diction: the students decided the cowboys would talk in absolutely ordinary language:

"Hot shower'll sure feel good," replied Frank D. They could ask: if I *didn't* put that down, what could I put down? General rule of thumb: drive the content inward if you can. I once assigned a group of students the job of describing the room we sat in. A volunteer said, "It has old painted walls now chipping, and the chairs are Early Good Will."

"That's the first thing you thought of," I said, "and it is accurately observed, too. Anyone else?"

Several people volunteered more details. Then someone said, "It doesn't look like a room where anything really classy would ever happen."

"Like what?" I said.

"Like people falling in love or anything."

We then chose two of the physical attributes of the room and added the inward comment that the room did not look like a place where anyone might fall in love. It made accurate prose about a gritty place—with the lift of the inward observation.

Plurals and Generics

There is a secret of writing which not only do beginners not know as a psychological law, but when someone tells them about it, they refuse to believe it. It is this: only a *singular* thing can be imagined by a reader or by oneself at any one given time. Only the *specific* can be cared for. Sociologists write without exception with plurals and generics: they want to make quick, all-inclusive summaries. They do not care if we *feel* the human experience of their content or not. Perhaps they prefer we stay cool, able to assimilate some more statistics. A sociologist's plan is for the reader to become a planner. A writer's plan is for the reader to be mortally touched.

Here is a demonstration of the psychological law: only one thing can be imagined at one time. Let us imagine that a hard day is over. We are sitting with people we like a lot or love, looking over the back garden. We are not forcing anyone to praise the Carpathian Harebells which were so hard to get started. We are respecting one another's quiet. Just now a red-trunked elephant comes smashing the stone wall between our back garden and the neighbor's. First its trunk sends chunks of rock and mortar flying. Soon the entire elephant is standing in our garden, its wrinkled ankles looking weary. Its eyes look as if it had spent all day estimating the thicknesses of things, to see what could be gone through and what couldn't.

Here is a second scene: both of us, you and I, have come nearly to the end of our unemployment payments—yours this week, mine on Thursday. We lean our elbows on the kitchen table. We are going through the same tripe we have been through a dozen times. "Maybe I could raise rabbits." "Maybe I could make handsewn hotpads with people's initials on them, as a yuppie fad that would catch on." "Maybe you and I together could drive to the South Dakota border and clean out some ag dealer's park-out inventory."

Just then your mother comes bursting into the house, without knocking—that horrible habit she has. I hear sirens behind her and think, Yes—if we tried to steal we'd get caught because we aren't skilled at it. Your mother is grinning. "Hurray, my sweeties! Take it! I must fly!" She takes an ugly old valise and dumps it upside down on the flannel-backed plastic cloth. Out comes $14,000 in ones. $14,000! And she has clattered through the house and out the back door. You, moving faster than I, arm all that money into a garbage bag under the sink.

There are two scenes. Now try to imagine both at exactly the same time—the red elephant sizing up for another wall-smashing, and Mom coming through when needed. They can't be seen at once.

Therefore: have *as few plurals as possible* in fiction. Sociologists tell us millions will die if such and such happens. We feel nothing because millions is very plural.

This brings us to a second idea: we don't feel much with *generics*, either. "Millions will die! Millions!" shouts the sociologist. If we ask her, "How many kids have you got?"

"Two," she says. "Why?"

"What are their names?" we ask.

"James and Ellen."

"OK" we say. "Will James and Ellen die? You suggested people like James and Ellen will die—if—what was it?"

Her face changes. She pictures two specifics: James and Ellen, her children, dead. Pirandello wrote a beautiful short story called "War" which depends entirely on a wise old man suddenly imagining a *specific* death. Specifics—even proper names, brandnames—make all the difference.

Here are two passages of plural-and-generic literature and their cures.

Plural and Generic Example #1

Night after night I pigged out and then joined friends for recreation.

Analysis

What are all the plurals? What are all the generics? Night after night is plural in *time*. Plural time is as boring as plural objects. That is why fairy tales start with "Once upon a time . . . " instead of "Now this just kept happening, year in year out."

Friends is plural: pigging out and recreation are generic. We don't know what got eaten or what the recreation was. So here is the improved version.

Improved

On October 14th, 1987, I pigged out on two fried bananas, one orange, and half a dried apricot I found at the Higgins Quicky Counter. Then Joanne, Merv, Belcher and I met under the marquee. We sat through *Anna Karenina* twice.

Plural and Generic Example #2

Old age is a diminished circumstance unless one converts former physical prowess into psychological or spiritual acumen. In fact, the more decrepit people are physically, the more elevated their souls need to become now.

Improved

An aged man is but a paltry thing—
A tattered coat upon a stick unless
Soul clap its hands and sing, and louder sing
For every tatter in its mortal dress[1]

Anglo-Saxon and Latinate Language

George Orwell's essay "Politics and the English Language" (so generally anthologized I won't give a book reference here) is so good and thorough on when not to use Latinate language and what happens if writers use more Latinate language and less Anglo-Saxon language that I suggest every short-story writer own and study a copy of the essay. I suggest even that everyone memorize a few of the horrible examples George Orwell gives—since those horrible examples are still much in use. As long as horrible language is in our ears, we have to stand picketline against letting any of it *in*.

We cannot count on our writing teachers to help us clean our language of extra Latinates, because our teachers, by 1990, have been brought up to Latinates. We even have creative-writing teachers using expressions like "I can relate to that" and "your story shows positive sharing of numerous concerns." Don't trust anyone who is willing to use dead language without even stumbling.

It is helpful to know a little of how Latin-based and German-based words coagulate in our language. Here, therefore, is a lightning sketch: A FOUR-MINUTE HISTORY OF LATINATE AND ANGLO-SAXON IN THE ENGLISH LANGUAGE[2]

The Romans invaded Celtic Britain. The Romans held the part of Britain now called England and some of Scotland, holding off attacks from rough Saxon invaders for about three hundred years. The Roman soldiers spoke Latin, of course: the people they conquered were Celts. The people who began attacking Roman Britain from east and north were generally Nordic barbarians.

Roman presence in Britain didn't leave much Latin imprint on our language. There are dozens of place names—London from Londinium, but few words. Do-it-yourselfers as far from Britain as the San Francisco Bay Area knew enough to order their nails by penny-sizes: 8d nails for one-inch boards, 16d and 20d for 2x4s, and so on. The little *d* used to mean penny as late as February of 1973 in England and still lives in American lumberyards. It is an abbreviation for *denarius*, the Roman soldiers' bottom-value coin.

In the third and following centuries, the northern invaders took over Roman England. They were Anglo-Saxons (Saxons and Angles and other very rough peoples as well). Their language, following the fractal pattern of languages, changed from its various Germanic sources to what we call Old English. It was the language of *Beowulf* and *The Seafarer*.

In 1066 the French took England. Now they were the conquerors, thus the boss-people: anyone who happened to be selling eggs on the day before the battle of Hastings had the same hens still laying the day after. That person needed to sell the eggs somehow, whether to Englishpeople or Frenchmen. The poultry purveyor learned some French.

Government is organization. Its words are *system* words, whereas in private life, most talk is about *things*, even if we do reconnaissance of systems. Example: "Dear, would you please not track in mud?" To herself: Domestic felicity seems to require that I make the same individual requests for consideration repetitively without saying, "There you are, enacting your proclivity for inattention to how your dirt impacts on our habitation."

In government, when someone is annoyed at someone else's behavior, one casts the conversation into *abstractions, keeping the particular out of it as long as possible.* Example: "We register your concern about the border tensions. Please know we are persevering in negotiations to ameliorate all inequities, negative practices, indeed any injustices, however inclement the increment of tradition."

We make our way through such a passage, finally getting a translation:

"We see you are furious that our people keep crossing the border and tearing up the towns on your side, stealing everybody clean, etc. We mean to keep talking to both sides in order to quit the unfair, gross incidents, including those which, although cruel, have been going on so long they are beginning to feel natural to people."

After the French invaded England, the abstract language of government and thinking about organization—indeed most abstract thinking—gradually became French. George Orwell explains how to recognize Latinate words at a glance.

It gave our language the melodious, polysyllabic long-sentences of the French. That decorous language lay on top of the short, consonant-riddled words of Old English. By the time of Chaucer, Old English was well-mixed with French. We call such fourteenth-century English, Middle English.

Since most of our abstract words are Latinate, through the French, and most of our concrete words are Germanic, we have a two-toned language. We are lucky. Like all luck, it can be used for good or ill. Abstract language can be deliberately used to hide the true human meaning of what's being said— "Remove structures and enemy personnel" when what's meant is "Bomb those houses full of Vietnamese civilians."

Abstract language is gaily, voluptuously, used by social climbers. "We must exercise circumspection and in every instance, preserve our heritage and facilitate a gracious future for our descendants." That remark, which translates to "We're going to watch for the main chance so we can keep what *we've* got now for us and our children," has the pomposity dear to social climbers.

Abstract language is used by crooks in order to deceive

people unused to abstract language. No matter how closely a business fool, such as I am, reads the fine print of an insurance policy, I don't get the sense of it. I expect such language is partly crooked, on the part of the insurers, but another motivation, I think, is the plain fun of it. It is fun to set up abstract contracts. Then lawyers can make their interpretations of those abstractions and try to beat each other out—in an exciting arena—the law court. (Writers have a hard time remembering that almost every human practice has two or more motivations: we need to see them *all* as well as we can guess.)

In summary then: people use abstract language when

1. They want to hide moral meaning or emotional intensity.

2. They want to sound scientific and/or formal.

3. They want to sound classier than they usually sound (and aren't classy enough to know that abstractions mark you as *not* classy).

4. They want to deceive readers and listeners.

5. They want to have fun.

There is one more common use of abstractions. They appear in the first drafts of every essay or story I (and others I conferred with) try to write. Perhaps because our elementary-school teachers urged us to be formal, perhaps because we hear junk-language on public media, expressions like "purchase" instead of "buy." It is hard to be concrete and brief. I advise forgiving yourself for Latinate phrases in any first draft—but don't fail to replace them with chunkier English in the second.

Too much Anglo-Saxon language is not wonderful, either. The strength of Robert Herrick's famous poem to Julia about her clothes is all its Anglo-Saxon concrete detail and then, dropped in beautifully like a river flow in dry-boulder terrain, the Latinate "liquefaction" of her clothes. Hemingway used both Anglo-Saxon and Latinate words most of the time: it gave both steady rock and light elegance to his language.

A postscript to this brief discussion: when only Latinate abstractions are used, *things*, not people, are the subjects of sentences, and the verbs get thrown into the *passive voice*. (Note the sentence you just finished reading: subject Latinate abstractions and *things*; verbs "are used" and "get thrown." Social scientists like such usage: it feels scientific to them—a feeling left over from high-school days when the teacher tells us to write in our lab records: "Sulphur was added" or "Catalyst caused precipitation." So we would learn that we, human beings, are nothing and must stay out of the discussion. For every morally grown-up social scientist like Ernest Becker there likely are tens of thousands of sociologists who love that impersonal construction: "Feelings were felt by the participants in the circumstance."

People who want to make literature need *people* as the subjects of most sentences, and verbs should be in the *active*, not the *passive*, voice. Having people for the subjects of sentences stops much habitual lying. Here is a remark I have heard made about dozens of committee meetings: "There was obvious excitement and commitment to the project." I have been at meetings and then read, with amazement, that remark in the valuations. If the secretary or the evaluator or whoever wrote it were forced to use *people* as the subjects of the sentences, he or she would have to write:

"The participants were excited about and committed to the project."

That is much harder to say. Fear makes us write mealy English: when I am afraid, I write mealy English. It is helpful to notice if you are feeling afraid so you can watch that the language doesn't turn to melody and oil. It helps to keep some Horrible Examples around. Get hold, if you can, of the Rationale for Need of a really irresponsible community-arts or humanities project: there will be a Latinate, passive-voiced, and melodious slick of English almost worth memorizing. Failing that, look at the college-president's speech (a real one) which Donald Hall unearthed and has preserved forever in *Writing Well*.

Soft or Stale Words

I have discussed some stale language earlier in this handbook. Here is a short list of soft and stale words. In some cases, these words were once all right, but now have been worked or wrongly used for such a long time they are limp.

Dead Words	Their True Meanings
concerns	Angers, terrors, mild anxieties, large anxieties
negative	Unfavorable, disapproving, sad, infuriated, ominous
positive	Fortunate, happy, approving, favorable, receptive
deal with	Bear, negotiate, survive, cope
relate to	Love, like, understand, empathize, feel compassionate towards
bottom line	Underlying principle, crux, half-hidden priority
supportive	This cliché is so repellent to me I can't ever make my mind even try to think what it means.

The following words are simply weak. Writers have to do a personal revolution in order to get free of weak words: *chat, chuckle, abound, muse* (as a verb), *thrilled, unique, boundaries, centered, excited* (this word was all right until about 1970: then grants people got hold of it. Project directors without exception(!) told board members, national endowments, how "excited" they were about their feasibility studies, their projects, their outcomes), *effective, real* (ungrammatically used as an intensifying adverb), *quote* (as a noun), *skills* (especially in *writing skills*), *committed, commitment.*

The best plan is to give up using any of the words above. Don't waste time resisting the totalitarian command to give them up: just give them up the way one gives up short bowing when the violin teacher tells you to. Art is art and requires apprenticeship, doing work well because the teacher is watching you. If you give up ever using the word "concern" or "concerns" in the meanings above, or in the old 1950s meaning of the word meaning "large corporation" (a drugstore was not a concern, but the United States Steel Corporation was), you will find your ear sharpened for junk-language. You won't want it any more. If a model had never been told not to wear runny stockings, she might wear them all her life and wonder why she didn't give a perfect impression. Eschewing runny stockings will not spoil her éclat; using clean language will not wreck your verve and insight.

One of the ways which fiction writers use to suggest that a fictional character is stupid is to give that character U.S.A. junk-language:

Applicant for help: "O ma'am! sir! please help! I'm in horrible shape!"

Stupid character: "I hear your concerns, but we need to touch base and check out our procedures."

That piece of dialogue carries this message in symbol: a nice person in horrible need is being staved off by a bureaucrat who pretends he or she is going to help—but there will be a huge delay.

See how unlike life art is: in real life, there *are* social-services machinery and a good social worker *must* use the machinery because it has been shown to provide competent help in most cases, and it prevents misuse. It is a perfectly sound, realistic use of what the ethical genius, John Rawls, would call "rule of practice."[3]

In literature, however, junk-language dialogue is a device to present a "stupid character." An honest reader will confess the person seemed cold and dumb. Note the speeches which Tolstoy gives Karenin—not to jeer at him the way small minds jeer at people who have been cuckolded, but to show Karenin as a man terribly dependent on a *system-based* persona.

Long and Short Sounds

Long vowels or syllables ending with two consonants make slow, emphatic English: short vowels with scant consonance make flimsy English. In fiction, we use the difference between long and short syllables in two ways that I know of (perhaps there are several):

1. We fill passages in which we want beauty with many long sounds, and

2. We give short syllables with few clear ending consonants to charaters who are meant to have no self-confidence.

The real-life psychology involved is that people with low self-esteem *do* use shorter vowel sounds and less enunciation of consonants than their more confident confrères. If you listen carefully to people who don't think their ideas amount to much, you'll hear that they say fast and sketchily whatever they mean to say. Even when they say a word like "yeah," they don't draw it out: it comes out "yuh" fast, or even with imploded *t* to shorten the *uh* even more to "yut!"

I have vomited a lot on the North Sea, as have thousands during night crossings between Harwich and Kristiansand, Norway. That being so sick and also cold, though it was summer, tripled my respect for Norwegians who sailed dinghies and fishingboats from Norway down to England during World War II to join the Allied Forces. They had so much to be afraid of, and often, such small hope that the Air/Sea Rescue people would have received their radio cries and would have a destroyer or a submarine at the right place along their path. I wanted to describe such young people once: I was excited just by my own admiration for them. I decided to do what I could in physical sound. (You remember how Dylan Thomas said he practiced his craft or art not for the ivory stages, nor for the monumental dead, but for lovers who held the griefs of all the ages in their arms?) Just one time at least, I practiced mine for escaping Norwegian Underground people. I decided to use as many long vowels as I could:

> . . . the little sailing boat in the North Sea, with its crew young and beautiful; the sea had misted crystal into their handknitted caps and sweaters; their hands had chilled on the sheets and stays and tiller; their knees ably took the sea's heave—and all the time, the three of them kept looking and looking, hoping and half-knowing a powerful friend would emerge from the deep, come up alongside, and save them.[4]

I learned this notion of paying attention to sound from Allen Tate: he was impressed by D.H. Lawrence's use of mellifluous names for the derby winners in "The Rocking-Horse Winner": "Malabar!" Paul shouted—his last winner—just before he died. Tate made us student writers notice the "liquid" sounds (*l* and *r*). It was a poet's gift to story-writing students.

CHAPTER NINE: NOTES

1. W.B. Yeats, "Sailing to Byzantium."

2. I shall always be grateful to Professor John Clark, of the University of Minnesota English Department, who gave a one-hour lecture at some point each year to his Old English class, on how Latin-based and Saxon-based words got stirred, dropped out, or woven together. This four-minute history is based on Professor Clark's lecture.

3. John Rawls, "Two Rules of Justice," *A Theory of Justice*, Harvard University Press, 1971.

4. Carol Bly, "Talk of Heroes," *Backbone*, Milkweed Editions, Minneapolis, MN, 1985.

Our Tottering Plot

Solving for Plot Among Our Mixed Bag of Characters

In short-story writing, more plot is more: it is easy to cut too clumsy, too full a cast of characters or too various a set of scenes and happenings. It is much harder to invent than to cut. It is even harder to cull from one's own autobiography than to cut. Let us say we have always known that, so we let ourselves mountain up a pile of people. Even in this book, which is text, not short story, we have a huge *Dramatis Personae*:

Jill, an indifferent creative-writing student

Henry, her boyfriend with an interest in geology

LaVonne, an unpleasant woman cross at her husband on their anniversary because he's late coming home

Vern Schwach, LaVonne's husband, a whistle-blower in a chemical-warfare laboratory

LeRoy, a Unocal 76 lessor whose Labrador bitch has been stolen

Don, a batterer, and Kate, his wife, who live near the Unocal 76, halfway between St. Paul, Minnesota, and St. Fursey Lake, Minnesota

Peter Tenebray, an Andover and Yale graduate, head of a science institute where research on chemical warfare is being conducted with Defense Department funding

Natalie, his wife, an alcoholic with very nice parents

John, a friend of Peter's from his college's secret society, Bercelius

Silver, a Labrador bitch

Mrs. Schwach, Vern's mother, who saves the dog's life

Natalie Tenebray's parents

Doc Buchwald, a vet in St. Fursey Lake

Dieter, an old Nazi, who helps on LaVonne's dad's strawberry farm

LaVonne's dad

Kate's father

LeRoy's rich missionary cousin (by mention only)

Bunt, a bartender

Angela Blackbury, a biochemist

Duane Salaco, a tough lab supervisor, who works for Peter Tenebray, fires Vern

Chuck, a carburetion student on a blind date in the backseat of the car

Too many characters is more blessing than worry. As Badger told Mole in their cozy discussion of underground housing (*The Wind in the Willows*, by Kenneth Grahame), if you find you've got too much, you've only got to stop up a tunnel or two. If you want more later, a dig and a scratch, and there you are.

In our inadvertent story, we have dozens of fragments, thematically unconnected it seems. Here is where many plot-writers make a mistake. They decide the story is poorly connected, far too coincidental, and that it certainly lacks unity. They begin to cut out characters. They feel pressed to solve for plot: as in algebra, they want to factor out and cancel what they can. Good heavens, who needs that bartender, Bunt? they ask themselves, and cross a line through his name. Natalie Tenebray can complain to someone else, they think.

They are right to realize it must all be condensed, but the only psychologically acceptable way to condense a list of characters is to find out and save whichever characters carry the most emotion for *you* the author. I find this out in two ways so far. There must be better procedures; these two are what I've thought of so far:

1. I write a family-systems "mapping" for each character

2. I write a little biography for each character starting with the present time of the story, going forward until that character's death and including the death.

Mapping

Mappings are lists shown like graphs. You put the name of the character in the center of a whole sheet of paper. Around the edges of the paper, you write the names of all the people in that character's life. Next, you draw a solid line radiating from the character out to any of the peripheral names of major im-portance to the character. You can code these solid lines with hatching for bad or hurtful influence. Then you draw a broken line out to people who simply "service" the character in some practical way: e.g., if I were doing a mapping of the character Vern Schwach, I would put in a hyphenated line between him and LeRoy the Unocal 76 dealer, since LeRoy (at least at the beginning of the story) only fills Vern's gas tank and wipes his windshield. I would draw a strong, hatched line between Vern and the tough lab supervisor who fired him. I would draw a hyphenated line between the lab supervisor (if we are doing a mapping of him) and Peter Tenebray: they are only colleagues, at different levels, in impersonal work.

Let's say that I have been really thoroughgoing and have done a careful mapping for *each* character. What would the good of that be?

1. It forces me to see *other*: e.g. in Silver's life, the strong lines go between herself and LeRoy, the hyphenated lines go between herself and Doc Buchwald, who to her is only someone LeRoy takes her to for shots, a hatched line goes to whoever stole her and dropped her off on I-35.

2. Mapping indirectly orients us in our appropriate subject matter. How can I not notice, for example, that as I map out the people's lives in this rough-and-tumble text-story, that not one of all the *Dramatis Personae* has as his or her major motivation physical love? Not one of those twenty-one people! Not even Silver, the dog! Not even Jill and Henry, who affectionately read geology textbooks together. The cast of the mapping gives its irrefutable message: this author, for at least this time and in this piece of fiction, is not likely to write passages which will topple grateful readers into their best memories of joy. Too bad. C.S. Lewis, who was so touchy about sex, gave an evening's furry love-scene to two bears in the third book of his Christian fantasy trilogy. Well, we don't read C.S. Lewis for good sex scenes. The lesson of mapping is to scan it for what it can tell us of our own *heart's truth*, although the mapping is superficially about the characters. It saves us making the conventional mistake of saying, "O but other writers write about physical desire: I'd better get some in." It also saves us from doing research on a subject which might feel forced. I am so glad that Louisa May Alcott didn't feel constrained to use Meg-and-John-Brooke or Amy-and-Laurie-Lawrence or Jo-and-Friedrich-Bhaer as subjects of

conjugal passion. We don't read C.S. Lewis or Amy Tan[1] (nor Alcott, of course) for passages about desire; yet beginning writers often feel forced to put in physical passion.

It is typical of our western culture that authors don't feel pressed to put in public, ethical considerations. I think it is very odd that we have no great body of stories about nice Bryn Mawr and Wellesley graduates who feel a little shaken, as they night after night climb into bed with men who frankly protect one another legally from getting caught in huge government frauds. It must be strange to live intimately with such men. We know that some tens of thousands of women do, yet I don't know of a single serious author telling those women's stories. I don't know of writers' conferences where teachers tell students, "You've got to get in something about ethical anxiety." No one complains that Alice Munro's stories do not include any about high-level organization of human beings for the purpose of polluting Canadian air or desiccating Canadian forest for profit. The Munro of "Royal Beatings" has her own ethical anxiety.

We don't press Munro for what's not her natural material. Nor should we press ourselves for what isn't our material. Mapping shows us which interests we have not got—which coastlines we don't study charts for because we don't mean to sail along them.

But the issues in mapping are two, not one: mapping should reveal natural subjects, but it can also rouse us to look at heretofore unconsidered subjects which we *should* look at. If we think back how Jill wrote obvious interludes about a couple making-out in the gravel pit, it is clear she could have benefitted from doing a mapping of herself and of all her characters. She would have moved her characters indoors to a Barnes & Noble Bookstore, and then she would have made at least some of the characters *her* kind of people—shy, a little bookish, angry at "foreclosed"-minded parents, ready to live an imaginative life . . . full of pity for things ill-used. How much more quickly Jill would have found the literary corner she could write best in! Let's consider again the Wellesley woman loyally married to someone who does bad work in our world: let's make her a person of good will, not a villain. Let's say she is not in it for money and social position. Let's say that her philosophy of marriage is loyalty, and "leave the workplace to him—he's man enough. He doesn't need for *her* to weigh in with criticism when he comes home exhausted. Besides, she and other people like her keep half the arts organizations going in their city. True, she slicks up her lateral reach at the net both left and right with her tennis pro, but that's all of one morning a week, thank you very much! What do *you* do every Tuesday at 10 a.m.? Tie yourself to a nuclear submarine?"

Let's tentatively add up all the Ivy League colleges which women attend in this way: we estimate the total number of graduates each year; then we estimate a total for all graduates from 1940 to 1968. (In the age group of those classes, males came to take nearly all high-level corporate positions.) Then we estimate how many of all those graduates married men who became executives in major organizations which did any of the following:

1. Electromagnetic, chemical, noise, or effluent pollution

2. Irresponsible desiccation, foresting, mining, or other depletion

3. Destabilized foreign countries economically so they had to produce in the way which made their country most profitable for American business

(Let's limit the men to those three activities.) Surely, at least three or four times each, in those years, some hundreds of those wives must have deplored what their husbands' organizations did.

If as few as twelve of them grieved twelve times each, and somehow those twelve people did a family-systems eco-mapping, we would see their distress as a pattern of sadness which ought to appear in American literature.

A last word on how mapping shows us truths by what's missing in the mapping. In our cast of characters from this book, there are no people who do evil *consciously just be-cause it works*. The evil-doing characters are:

1. Peter Tenebray

2. Duane Salaco

3. Donny (a wifebeater)

4. An unnamed dog stealer and dropper

Not one of these people is a current Iago of the savings and loan fraud. I have to realize, a little grimly, that there is small chance I will be able to write a short story in which sympathetic characters do major stealing from the American people of the present and of the future. I don't seem to know the people. But I can imagine people at Kohlberg's Moral Reasoning Stage II; that is, people for whom loyalty to pals is more vital than the public concern.

To succeed, a major fraud seems to need hundreds of people whose motivation *not to offend or turn in friends and pals* is greater than their honor towards invisible impact groups (the rest of us in the American economy now and for years to come, in the case of the savings and loan fraud). *The New York Times* quotes Charles A. Bowsher, the Comptroller General, as saying, "This is a huge scandal, and to a large extent it was allowed to grow because of the way this town does business." The author of the article, David E. Rosenbaum, goes on to observe that

> The Carter, Reagan and Bush Administrations, eager to avoid bad economic news or measures that would throw budgets further out of balance . . . were never taken to task by their opponents . . . Many of the most powerful people in Congress were blinded by friendships with savings and loan executives at home and their quest for campaign donations from an industry that had deep pockets.[2]

Obviously, how the rich as well as the poor put their own friends ahead of *invisible victims* needs to show up in American fiction. In his stage-development theory for moral reasoning, Lawrence Kohlberg[3] assigns the second of his two "pre-moral" stages to people who (at the time of assessment) have as their main ethic getting what they can for themselves, but realizing that others naturally do the same, and thus they are sports about letting them do it. It is the college-graduate version of the tolerance between New York streetgangs whose purlieus do not overlap.

Just for the interest of people unfamiliar with Kohlberg's ingenious stages, here is a very simple reduction:

Stage 1. Lowest (pre-moral): everything for self. If there is some behavior that works out well for me, that behavior is judged *good*. A baby is at stage one when it suckles its mother. Suckling is *good*.

Stage 2. (Still a pre-moral stage.) Awareness that others have their wants: therefore, we make deals between us to pre-vent overlap of resource-territories, and our attitude towards these selfish others is: they're like me, that's how it goes, this is reality, hey. This stage, too, is "pre-moral."

Stage 3. Good behavior is behavior which brings strokes from peers. This is the stage of teenagers who pretend to like rock when they prefer Haydn and of small-town Kiwanians who do seasonal fund-raising because seasonal fund-raising makes you OK with your peers, who are always the powers that be. Whatever is coming down, you go with it, in order not to be different, in order to receive reinforcement.

Stage 4. Good behavior is obedience to whatever your sovereign group assigns as good behavior. If you are an Ameri-can, and this is 1967, you do your duty and join American forces. This fourth level (like the third level just before it) is *conventional*: people thinking at this level check with peers and with authority to see what they should think is good. The Vietnam War's veteran, defending himself from then-protestors, exclaiming, "Well, I got to serve my country, don't I?" is the *cri de coeur* of Stage Four thinking.

Stage 5. Good behavior is the behavior one has thought through for oneself. Stage 5 is the first better-than-conventional stage.

Stage 6. In Stage 6, one recognizes *universal application* of what is fair: if it is unfair to cheat people, then it is unfair to cheat them *anywhere*. One's foreign policy, if one is a Stage Six person, would not be to grant certain *rights to Americans* but devil take the hindmost so far as foreign countries (especially Third-World countries) are concerned.

If we return to our cast of characters we can see how Kohlberg's stages have their participants, but not on the grand scale nor with the panache of savings and loan defrauders:

Our most-advantaged person is Peter Tenebray, who runs his unpleasant business at profit to himself with the ethical grasp of a Stage 4 person: Peter's sovereign group, the United States, through its Defense Department, wants chemical-warfare savvy. Peter exercises fealty. Peter's allegiance to the sovereign group overwhelms whatever scruples he feels as he watches the animals writhe in their lab cages.

His lab supervisor, Duane Salaco is absolutely pre-moral: he is at Stage 1 or Stage 2, as we see, if we go back and listen again to his conversation with Vern Schwach as he fires Vern.

Donny, the wifebeater, is either absolutely pre-moral (simply doing whatever gives himself profit—in a used-car lot—or pleasure—sadistically abusing his wife) or he is a true Iago: a person devoted to evil purpose consciously. We would have to think him through—and decide.

The fourth of the evil-doers in our cast is the unknown dog-stealer. We needn't think him or her through unless we decide to do much more with that character.

The mapping we do will give us an idea, then, not only of our *interest* but of our *scope*. Our cast of characters here are not powerful or very rich people. Peter probably has the top salary: he gets $90,000 from the Institute job, plus $100,000 or $200,000 from his portfolio, the portfolio swelled by his mother's holdings at her death. LaVonne Schwach probably has the smallest income: she works two days a week vacuuming around Doc Buchwald's veterinary office and lab, filling two K-type bags with cat hair each time: it relieves the boredom of her St. Fursey life.

After we have decided what we *won't* try to bring in from outside our natural purview, we need to distinguish among all the people we already have on scene. A great way to do that is to write up their lives from now until their deaths, so we can see whom we are interested in and whom not.

Planning the Eventual Death of Each Character for Plot Use and for Our Own Psychological Clarity

This discipline of making oneself write up the characters' futures is less eccentric and more useful than it looks. Here's an example. My first instinct would be to toss out the friend of Peter Tenebray's named John. John doesn't amount to much in our material so far: he is some sort of colleague of Peter's, but with another organization loosely federated with Peter's. He is another old Yale man, actually from the same Secret Society. Who needs him? I thought, petulantly looking over the cast to see how to make my *plot* job easier. In my imagination, I float various deaths towards John, trying them for size. If I decide that John already knows he has a terminal disease, I then see that he might likely tell Peter sharper truths than otherwise.

But I wrote his life to the end and realized that I wanted him for the person who would put it up to Peter that what Peter was doing was not acceptable. I made Peter offer him a marvelous job—piles of money and perks of various kinds, involving sitting on some blessedly inactive Boards which pay but don't need you. This figure, John, gave me a *good* voice out of Peter's background. It gave me a chance to show how higher-up gentlemanly types get fired, too. We all know how lab bosses fire people like Vern Schwach. How does someone like Peter Tenebray fix it so John will be very, very sorry he tangled with Peter and tried to make Peter lose face? (Peter *would* see being told his work was immoral primarily as face-losing.)

If I try writing various deaths for Don or for Kate, I might find that death has too much heft for those characters, which tells me that in my mind they are minor characters, and I mustn't force them to major action. It also tells me this: not to go inside such a character with prolonged interior monologue. If I don't love the person enough to make her death sit firmly on her, then I don't love her enough to hear her inward voice.

When I write up the future of Silver, I realize I want her back. I now confirm that Mrs. Schwach found her dragging along the side of I-35 and took her in to what someone said was the nearest vet, and the vet recognized LeRoy's bitch. Happy ending. Why not? Sad endings are a cliché.

The prospect of writing up these to-the-death stories makes me realize I should like to drop the following people or combine them with each other or with others:

> Chuck the horrible blind date could just as well be Donny on his first date with Kate. We can then make the "I" of the blind-date scene Kate.

> LeRoy's rich missionary cousin is absolutely nothing. His dialogue about her is drivel, too. It's a chance to drop her.

> Dieter, the old Nazi, is rather a nice figure, especially now it is all coming out so very publicly how the U.S. re-established so many Nazis just after World War II in order to help do high-tech sabre-rattling at the Soviet Union in 1945–1980. I should hate to drop Dieter, but he doesn't fit in much of anywhere. If we have to, we can combine him with someone, but not the vet because I like the vet too much. Dieter might have to wait for another story.

And so forth. Soon both the themes and the cared-for characters will make themselves clear. New scenes emerge. We could get Peter and Natalie, and John, whom Peter is wooing for some joint Defense Department project, up to St. Fursey for a lovely fall weekend by the water. A good many events seem to be taking place:

> It is LaVonne's and Vern's anniversary.

> Mrs. Schwach will save Silver, and Doc Buchwald will tell LeRoy to pick her up at his animal hospital.

Kate and Don enact another of the terrible crises of their marriage.

Peter Tenebray has perhaps very self-righteously decided not to start up a little something with Angela Blackbury— he commends himself for this, as he has a right to: it is hard not to follow where desire promises so much. It is twice as infuriating to Peter, therefore, to be told down by his old pal John all weekend, stuck up there in the woods—*and with Natalie plastered again of course.*

Natalie wanders off from the resort.

It is at this point that Henry James is so ingenious: he would cast his eye down the list of people and realize that there is a chance to have a Long-Lost-But-Now-Propitiously-Returning person come back. Who? Of course—the daughter of Donny and Kate, who ran away after Donny called her a whore for getting pregnant. She needs a name. Phyllis.

Like Mrs. Schwach, Phyllis is at the motel and can't get up her nerve to get back into the rattletrap (a '74 Escort with zillions of miles on it and tailpipe assembly which makes it sound like a tank) and drive down to see her mama. The motel lady says, "Did you want another night or what?"—a little rudely, because of this young woman's manlessness and bad clothes.

I see what needs to happen here. The story is almost over, of course, but not everyone has had a chance to do anything nice for anyone else. Vern was very nice to LeRoy; he got him safely out of the VFW before that tough fellow, Don someone, got back at him. He even put a bandage on LeRoy's knuckles. But Natalie has not had a chance to do anything for anyone. She bemoans Peter's life decisions and drinks.

She needs to meet up with Kate and Donny's daughter, and help the young woman with the baby, and tell the baby, who is too young to listen, but whose mother isn't, about how this is a mysterious universe, and however grisly the outlook, something gorgeous might happen out there yet. There are, Natalie assures Phyllis, slurring her consonants but holding firm on her statistics, at least 450,000 people in this country alone who want something gorgeous to happen.

They sit on motel lawn chairs. Seagull droppings from St. Fursey Lake birds lie bright on the arms because the motel-owner explained, people steal her sheets so why should she wipe off the chairs which they've got so much leisure to sit on when she's on her feet all day, so fuck them, is her last word on the subject. Natalie gets to hold the baby, and Kate's daughter gets to hear that there are other species around this place besides human beings, for the love of God, and they're nicer. Natalie says, Phyllis, I'm taking us out to dinner. They go out to dinner. Natalie distinctly remembers when she was a kid in Duluth how a whole family of black bears, mom, dad or uncle, and a cub, moved in next door. She was only a little girl at the time, so she was afraid the bears wouldn't make it, but there were COACT people around and the neighbors pitched in.[4] Even Natalie's mother and father tossed a coin heads or tails to see who got to make a hot-dish for the bears and who had to take it over to them. Natalie's father won. He invented a casserole he hoped they would like: it was made of honey, blueberries, and Lake Superior Whitefish. Natalie's mother had to take it over.

Saving What Doesn't Fit

For all our struggles, some drafts of stories will not become stories. Sometimes we have worked up a piece of writing which will do for two essays, one novel, four poems, or simply a comparatively elaborate anecdote to tell at parlor games. Perhaps the story can serve as example of a Failed Story: we can tell or show it to student writers like Jill, so they will get the knack of doing the whole energetic process of plotting—and having it fail. Conversely, they will see how very near workable some manuscripts are which fail: they may go back to re-structuring an old story with new courage.

There is a point beyond which we can't help one another

with setting plot. That is because we must each follow our own best psychological instinct: mine drives me to want to get into fiction the harshest events of our time, because those harsh events are on my mind and because I want social change more than I want literature with unbroken skin around it. My philosophy says this to me all the time: we have had Virginia Woolf to show us that harsh truths belong in literature so that literature, like psychotherapy and social work, can be a profession which tries to help. If literature occasionally acts as a "helping profession," it means its authors love what's fair enough so they can write literature about what is not fair.

It seems like a lot to ask of an art form which depends on playful artifice. How can we stay playful and be profound? How can we tell our heart's truth and still have perspective enough to see that something quite *other* may be going on for someone else? How can we be scared that we may lose our planet with its snows and its morning fogs and its groves full of animals, yet still say: "Listen: the strangest thing happened . . . This woman was just sitting beside the lake, minding her own business, when . . . "

We can work away at tone and scope and plot. Our world needs better heart than we have given it so far. Stories can show that: they can show how touching the world is, and how we want to pour out a sort of literary kindness onto it, so it can turn in that kindness, the way it turns in the cold air.

CHAPTER TEN: NOTES

1. Amy Tan, *The Joy Luck Club*, Putnam, New York, 1989.

2. David E. Rosenbaum, "A Financial Disaster With Many Culprits," The *New York Times*, Wednesday, June 6, 1990, pp. A-1 and C-4.

3. Lawrence Kohlberg, *The Philosophy of Moral Development*, Vol. I, Harper & Row, New York, 1981.

4. COACT is a community action organization which enables citizens to identify and actively solve their communal problems. There are COACT linkages in various American cities. COACT is the epitome of grassroots effort against poverty and injustice.

Carol Bly's second collection of stories, *The Tomcat's Wife and Other Stories* (HarperCollins, 1991), won the Friends of American Writers Award. Five of her essays are included in *Eight Modern Essayists*, edited by William Smart (St. Martin's Press, 1990). She is the author of *Backbone*, her first book of short stories (Milkweed Editions, 1985), the essay *Bad Government and Silly Literature* (Milkweed Editions, 1987), and the acclaimed book of essays, *Letters from the Country* (Harper & Row, 1981).

Bly is the co-author of *Soil and Survival: Land Stewardship and the Future of American Agriculture* (with Joe Paddock and Nancy Paddock, Sierra Club Books, 1986). She was the Benedict Distinguished Visiting Professor of English at Carleton College (Spring 1990). Bly teaches Ethics at the University of Minnesota; she is a frequent lecturer, a humanities consultant to the Land Stewardship Project, and serves on the Board of Directors of the Loft. She received an honorary doctoral degree from Northland College in 1992. Carol Bly lives in Sturgeon Lake and St. Paul, Minnesota.

Interior design by Randy Scholes
Typeset in ITC Garamond
by Stanton Publication Services, Inc.
Printed on acid-free Booktext Natural paper
by BookCrafters, Inc.

More nonfiction from Milkweed Editions:

Changing the Bully Who Rules the World:
Reading and Thinking about Ethics
Carol Bly

Transforming a Rape Culture
Edited by Emilie Buchwald, Pamela Fletcher, and Martha Roth

Rooms in the House of Stone
Michael Dorris

The Most Wonderful Books:
Writers on Discovering the Pleasures of Reading
Edited by Michael Dorris and Emilie Buchwald

Boundary Waters:
The Grace of the Wild
Paul Gruchow

Grass Roots:
The Universe of Home
Paul Gruchow

The Mythic Family
Judith Guest

The Art of Writing:
Lu Chi's Wen Fu
Translated from the Chinese by Sam Hamill

Chasing Hellhounds:
A Teacher Learns from His Students
Marvin Hoffman

Coming Home Crazy:
An Alphabet of China Essays
Bill Holm

The Heart Can Be Filled Anywhere on Earth:
Minneota, Minnesota
Bill Holm

Shedding Life:
Disease, Politics, and Other Human Conditions
Miroslav Holub

Rescuing Little Roundhead
Syl Jones

I Won't Learn from You!
The Role of Assent in Learning
Herbert Kohl

Basic Needs:
A Year with Street Kids in a City School
Julie Landsman

Tips for Creating a Manageable Classroom:
Understanding Your Students' Basic Needs
Julie Landsman

The Old Bridge:
The Third Balkan War and the Age of the Refugee
Christopher Merrill

Planning to Stay:
Learning to See the Physical Features of Your Neighborhood
William R. Morrish and Catherine R. Brown

Homestead
Annick Smith

What Makes Pornography "Sexy"?
John Stoltenberg

Testimony:
Writers of the West Speak On Behalf of Utah Wilderness
Compiled by Steve Trimble and
Terry Tempest Williams